THE COMPLETE GUIDE TO SMALL GAME TAXIDERMY

ALSO BY TODD TRIPLETT

The Complete Guide to Turkey Taxidermy

THE COMPLETE GUIDE TO SMALL GAME TAXIDERMY

How to Work with Squirrels, Varmints, and Predators

Todd Triplett

The Lyons Press
Guilford, Connecticut
An imprint of The Globe Pequot Press

Dedication

This book is dedicated to my grandfather who took me on that first squirrel hunt and helped to ignite my burning desire to hunt. Thankfully, this fire has never been extinguished. And to my father, who helped me mount those first few critters and who taught me to appreciate wildlife art. Last, but certainly not least, I dedicate this book to the love of my life, Sherry. Without her, my desire to become a professional taxidermist and outdoor writer may never have become reality.

The Lyons Press is an imprint of The Globe Pequot Press.

ISBN 1-59228-145-1

Printed in [TK]

10 9 8 7 6 5 4 3 2 1

Design by [TK]

Library of Congress Cataloging-in-Publication data is available on file.

Contents

Acknowledgments

The art of taxidermy has moved forward by leaps and bounds in recent years. These advances have been primarily due to individuals bonding together to share information that was once a closely guarded secret. In the early days of taxidermy there were no books, videotapes, or schools. The only way a person could learn the art of taxidermy was through trial and error, lots of research, and—with luck—a close friend willing to share his knowledge. Without the help I received during the learning stages, I may have given up on taxidermy.

But as taxidermy evolved in the information age, so did the availability of learning material. Today, budding taxidermists can contact a variety of suppliers that have full-time taxidermists on staff to answer questions. They can also call upon the assistance of state and national taxidermy associations, which are usually more than glad to help a new taxidermist. And there are a variety of books and videos available.

So I'd like to thank the taxidermists who have been so willing to open the storehouse of taxidermy wisdom. Remember this when someone following in your footsteps comes to you for help.

Also, I must thank Scott, Justin, and Sherry for helping with the pictures for this book.

Introduction

I listened for my prey as I slipped quietly through the woods. The crunching of dry autumn leaves as a gray squirrel bounded from one tree to another was easy to recognize, even for an eight-year-old. Though I had tagged along on many squirrel hunts, this was the first trip on which I was allowed to carry my own shotgun.

The setting for this early safari was an old roadbed that coursed through the woodlot behind our home in the mountains of North Carolina. As I neared the end of the path, the sound of a bushy-tail scurrying about grew louder. I went into stealth mode, standing as still as a statue. After a brief wait, which seemed like an eternity, the gray squirrel made his way up a tree within sight of where I stood.

With the moment of truth at hand, I raised my grandpa's trusty 20-gauge, a beautiful Ithaca Model 37 that sported an engraving of a bird dog at work on the receiver. I pointed the smoothbore toward the fleeting gray streak, my heart pounding in my chest. At just the right moment I pulled the trigger. Luckily, the shot was true and the squirrel fell from the limb.

I ran to my prize. The corners of my smile seemed to touch each ear as I held that plump November gray. I remember the strong feelings that rushed through my mind. I was extremely excited at having made my first kill, but there was a pinch of remorse for the taking of a life. Both emotions remain with me to this day.

Granted, this wasn't Alaska or the mountains of Colorado, where my father had traveled many miles in pursuit of elk, mule deer, caribou, and moose. But it was still a very special time for me. Time spent with my grandfather, which I cherish to this day, and time spent in my favorite places, the fields and forests. This was *my* hunt, and after being successful I felt I was truly a part of the hunting world that I had so longed for.

The taking of that first squirrel also sparked my desire to learn taxidermy. Such knowledge was readily available to me, as my father was a taxidermist. But the motor skills of an eight-year-old proved less than suitable for the work at hand. Thinking I'd mount the gray squirrel, I quickly went to work skinning it. That notion was short-lived, however, as I soon had quite a mess in front of me. So I settled for a fried reminder of that hunt. Although I bungled my first attempt at taxidermy, I never lost my desire to complete a mount.

A year or so later I attempted to skin a dove I'd taken early in the fall. Needless to say, that was a bigger disaster than the squirrel. Obviously I didn't know it at the time, but a dove is one of the toughest birds to skin and mount. Yet I kept watching and trying to learn. Finally, at about the age of twelve, I completed my first mount, a jack-a-lope, as my father closely monitored my work. I don't know which was more enjoyable, the time spent with my dad collecting jackrabbits or actually completing the mount.

After a couple more seasons of hunting and taxidermy experience I was fortunate enough to harvest and mount my first deer. I still have that deer, a small spike, and each time I see it I recall that hunt as if it were yesterday. I also relish the fact that although it wasn't my finest work, it was the starting point that helped me reach where I am today.

As I developed into an experienced taxidermist, I noticed that no book on the market completely covered all aspects of small game or predator taxidermy. Sure, plenty of general taxidermy books were available, but none centered on any one species. Filling this niche seemed like a great way to pass along some of the techniques that I had been fortunate enough to learn through the years.

In addition to a broad range of general techniques for mounting small game, I'll discuss the details of mounting three specific animals: a squirrel, a bobcat, and a coyote. These projects—along with the rest of the information provided between these covers—will provide you with the skills and knowledge to mount any other small game you wish.

The techniques I describe in this book are simple, time-tested, and produce quality results. As you progress in the field of taxidermy, though, you will quickly find that there are many different techniques worth learning. And you'll eventually settle on the style that best suits you.

Whether you are setting out to become a world-class taxidermist, or simply want to learn how to mount your child's first squirrel, there is something here for you.

Small Game Field Care

S ince becoming a professional taxidermist, I have been asked to mount some horribly cared-for animals. The hunters who brought these animals in simply didn't understand the need for proper field care. From the hair on one side of a larger mammal being rubbed off during a drag to using too much gun for small game, I've had to deal with it all. The worst, though, is usually a wet animal that hasn't been stored properly.

When trophies are subjected to these harsh conditions, it obviously makes a tougher job for the person charged with re-creating this piece of wildlife art. Average hunters often don't give a second thought to the condition of their trophies when they leave them with the taxidermist. Yet they always wonder why the same animal appears less than perfect when the mount is completed.

The primary goal for any hunter who hopes to have his prize preserved should be to achieve the most impressive mount possible. And the best possible mount begins in the field with proper care of the trophy. Then, for the taxidermist, this same level of care should continue throughout the mounting process.

Proper field care should actually begin before a harvest even takes place, with proper preparation and planning. Even a highly skilled taxidermist won't be able to address every problem with an animal that's been poorly cared for. And trying to learn taxidermy on a less-than-perfect specimen will be nothing short of a disaster. It can be devastating to near the halfway point of the mounting process after a lot of work, only to have the hair begin slipping. Fortunately, taking the proper precautions will help reduce the risk of such an event.

Most hunters know before they venture afield whether or not they hope to preserve their prize, which is very helpful. It's also best to have a general idea of the pose you might want for the animal and where you will keep it after it's mounted. Once a hunter knows this, he can be extra cautious when dealing with certain areas of the mammal. For example, if a life-sized mount is chosen, then the entire skin will need to be closely cared for. But if a shoulder mount is the goal, obviously there's no need to be too concerned about anything beyond the head and shoulders. As many hunters go several seasons between harvests, taking extra steps early in the process will help ensure that your precious animal will be in the best possible shape for the desired mount.

A couple of years back a fellow was deer hunting when he suddenly had a chance to take a bobcat. As he was after deer, he was armed with a .30-06—a perfect deer rifle but tremendous overkill for a cat tipping the scales at a bit more than twenty pounds. This was the hunter's first opportunity at a bobcat, and he didn't even think about the devastating effect his shot might have. He quickly shouldered his rifle and pulled the trigger. At the crack of the gun the cat fell in a heap. The softball-sized hole on the opposite side of its body ensured instant death. The hunter was ecstatic. Upon retrieval, though, disappointment clouded his face as he spotted the huge hole.

The hunter rushed home and called me, explaining the details of his morning hunt. He asked if there was anything I could do to help. I told him to bring it over, and we could discuss the situation. Before he arrived I was thinking of the options we might have if the skin was damaged beyond repair—shoulder mount, half life-size, pedestal.

After examining the bobcat, I quickly discovered that all was not lost. Fortunately for the hunter, he had shot the cat almost perfectly in the center of the midsection. Because the skin in this area was flat, with no identifying marks, it seemed suitable for repair work. After skinning, I also discovered that the skin I thought had been ripped away was still there. It had simply been stretched outward as the bullet exited, then ripped into the form of a large "X." Several careful stitches later and the hole was gone.

Another hunter I know who found himself in a similar situation wasn't so fortunate. Also out hunting for deer, he too had the opportunity to harvest a highly prized bobcat. But instead of taking a body shot, which is always best for repairs, he opted for a head shot. The end result was that the damage was beyond repair.

Neither hunter knew what shot to choose for a repairable skin; the first hunter was simply more lucky.

Whether you're targeting them specifically or just luck into one, a bobcat makes a special trophy. Know where you need to place your shot for a quick, clean kill and a mountable, undamaged skin.

Though variables occur, there are some simple rules to follow for bringing home a prime taxidermy project. These include: avoiding major damage to the skin (especially in the facial area); keeping the hair or fur free of any fluids (including water or body fluids); and cooling the animal as soon as possible.

Avoiding skin damage can sometimes be tricky, depending on the weapon used and the given shot opportunity. The .22 caliber is an ideal weapon for small game, and it's preferable to use nothing larger than a .22 magnum. Most .22 magnums will cleanly take small game and predator-sized game out to seventy-five yards. Serious predator hunters who opt for something with more potency should stay in the .222 and .223 range. These larger calibers can reach out there, yet are much more friendly to skins than a .243. Also, the type of bullet used is important; a bullet that expands greatly isn't going to minimize skin damage.

For hunting squirrels or raccoons, where long-distance shooting isn't required, a shotgun works great. A shotgun with No. 6 shot will put several holes in a skin at moderate range, but most are so small

Proper field care will make it much easier to duplicate the beauty of the animals you hunt.

that no repairs will necessarily need to be made. The only drawback to having numerous small holes in the skin is that adhesive, if used, can get into the hair. In this situation, I would apply adhesive only to the head area.

Another key is keeping the hair and skin as dry as possible. While any bird or animal that is going to be mounted will likely be washed at a later time, it is best to maintain a completely dry trophy in the field. Blood and most other body fluids contain proteins that are tough to completely remove without using chemicals, or harsh washing. Moisture also aids unwanted bacteria growth.

To avoid getting blood on the hair of your trophy, take along cotton swabs or paper towels and plug any orifices. These include the mouth, anal opening, and any major shot hole that can be easily found. Certain circumstances are unavoidable. If you happen to get caught in a pouring rain or if an animal finds its way into a creek before expiring—and you have some taxidermy experience—the best thing to do is skin, flesh, wash, degrease (if needed), and dry the hair quickly using compressed air. Otherwise, you should try to get it into the freezer immediately.

While getting game to the freezer quickly doesn't seem difficult, even knowledgeable sportsmen often neglect to do it. The type of critter, along with the time of year it was taken, will influence how quickly you must act. A late-winter squirrel will be able to take much more abuse than an early-fall fox. That's not to say that you should be careless with the former, but some animals, as you will soon learn, withstand rough handling better than others. It has been my experience that foxes and coyotes are especially vulnerable to "slippage" problems. The worst areas seem to be the ears. For this reason it is best to get these animals skinned and preserved or salted without hesitation.

A mistake that comes back to haunt many a hunter is hauling the trophy around to show it to friends. At first, this problem doesn't seem as serious as it actually is. What you must understand is that heat and moisture are prime breeding grounds for bacteria, which is enemy number one to the taxidermist. And this detrimental bacteria begins growing the instant an animal dies. Even a critter in nearly perfect condition that's been otherwise properly cared for can be lost due to slippage from bacteria buildup.

It is certainly understandable why any successful hunter would want to show a trophy to his hunting buddies or coworkers, but this can have a decidedly negative effect later in the mounting process. The safest way to boast is to take several quality pictures, go to a one-hour photo center, and then visit everyone.

One more rule to follow is to skip the field dressing. This is most important if you're planning a life-sized mount. I am usually a fanatic for field dressing any game. But field dressing small game or predators destined for mounting usually creates more problems than it prevents. When you open up the animal in the field, more blood and fluids will be released to contaminate the hair.

Once a critter is successfully harvested and proper field-care guidelines have been followed you are almost finished with the first stage of preparation. If you have time to start the taxidermy work immediately, by all means continue. If not, proper storage should be your next priority. Do not put the trophy into a plastic bag right away, as this will help retain heat and may create moisture problems if the animal is still warm. Place the animal into a freezer without a bag for at least an hour, then remove and double bag to keep other freezer contaminants from getting on your prize. If freezer space is an issue, go through the skinning process detailed in chapter 4 and then place the skin in the freezer.

If you make the effort to carefully follow proper field-care procedures prior to mounting, you should be rewarded with a high-quality trophy that is a pleasure to work with.

Tools

As with any task, your foray into taxidermy will be more enjoyable if the right tools are available throughout the process. Some of these tools will seem pricey, but in the long run they are worth their weight in gold. While every tool might not be a must-have item when you are just starting out, buying the best possible tools will make certain tasks much simpler.

What follows is a description of each tool, what its duties are, and, in my opinion, whether it is optional.

Latex Surgical Gloves. I have seen numerous taxidermists over the years who neglected to use a glove of any kind while handling birds and mammals. Their usual reason for being so careless is that they can't feel their work as well. In my opinion, and in the opinion of most others in the field, this is without doubt a health bomb waiting to go off. When it comes to the issue of gloves, the only question should be, "What size do I need?"

While most diseases prevalent in the animal kingdom can't be passed to humans, some can. Rabies is probably at the top of the list. I know many taxidermists who will not even accept raccoons or foxes for this reason. Although the chances of ever coming into contact with a bird or animal that has a transmittable disease is probably somewhere between slim and none, it will be too late to consider your options once it happens.

Latex surgical gloves are definitely not optional.

Scalpel. This may be the most important tool of the taxidermy trade. The scalpel's duties are rather obvious: it's used to skin all birds and mammals. And while many hunters and taxidermists insist on a knife for skinning, using scalpels will remove the need to regularly sharpen a blade—and they are cheap when compared to the time it takes to keep a knife blade sharp. Scalpels also come much sharper

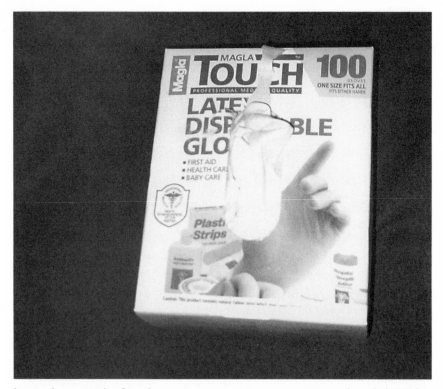

Latex gloves can be found at many convenience stores or purchased through a taxidermy supplier.

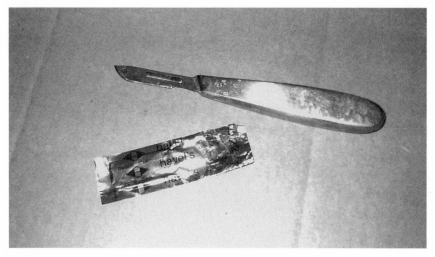

Scalpel with handle.

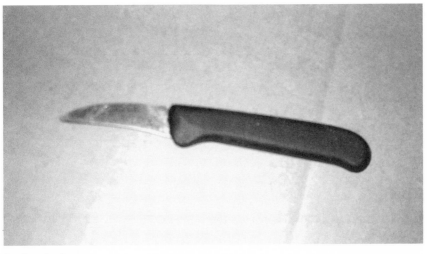

Perfect knife.

than you could ever hope to sharpen a blade by hand. Be extra cautious when using scalpels, though. Even the poorest grades are razor sharp, and a careless slip will quickly lead to a trip to the emergency room for stitches.

A scalpel can be used alone, but it is easier to manipulate when attached to a handle. While small plastic scalpel handles are available, I would advise that you invest an extra couple of dollars in a

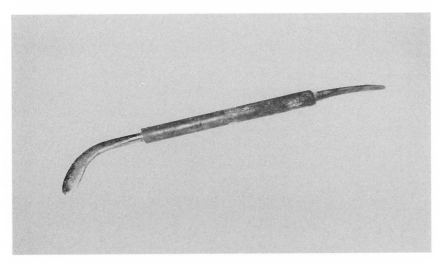

Sculpting tool.

weighted stainless steel handle. A weighted handle allows the scalpel to sit nicely in one hand while work is performed, and it will last a lifetime.

Scalpels are optional, but much more effective than knives.

Knives. Notice I've written "knives" and not "knife." While most beginners can start with a single knife, a supply of sharpened knives is beneficial for more advanced taxidermy work. Much of this work can be done with a supply of scalpels, but there are situations that may require a specialty knife; thick skins with larger areas to work, for example.

Many different knife designs are available, but I'd recommend starting with a blade in the three-inch range that is easily sharpened and maintains its edge. And remember, the adage "you get what you pay for" applies here.

Having at least one quality knife is mandatory.

Scissors. Small curved scissors can be used to trim around bullet holes or to reach otherwise inaccessible areas such as the base of the tail, or inside paws. Fat or muscle tissue can be very thin in places, holding tight against the skin. Small inexpensive scissors can be priceless in this situation.

Scissors are optional, but very useful for beginner and experienced taxidermist alike.

Sculpting Tool. A sculpting tool has many uses. Placing epoxy into shrunken areas, shaping the area around an eye, and shaping the interior of the nostrils during the mounting process are all things that can be done with a sculpting tool. And you will discover many other uses for this must-have tool.

Sculpting tools are usually available in plastic, wood, or stainless steel, but you can also shape the wooden end of a paintbrush into a sculpting tool. This allows you to shape with one end and clean up and blend with the other. If you can only afford one sculpting tool I would recommend the stainless steel version, as it will last forever. But it helps to own a few different designs in a variety of materials, which will allow you to match a specific design to a specific task.

Fleshing Beam. Fleshing beams range in size from models that mount to a workbench (these are the most popular, particularly for small game) to four-foot-tall floor models. A beam is used to support a skin so that it can be fleshed by hand. Even if you use a machine for the bulk of the fleshing process, a beam is still useful for hard-to-reach areas. For small game, a fleshing beam can also be used as the sole tool for fleshing if the taxidermist so desires.

Skife Knife. This "knife" is just a razor blade with a guard attached. It was developed to prevent excessively cutting the skin during fleshing. It is available from taxidermy suppliers and can be helpful for anyone still in the learning stages. The skife knife is optional.

Fleshing Machine. While you can flesh most small game and predators with a knife, scalpel, scissors, and a fleshing beam, you'll achieve better, quicker results with a fleshing machine.

Two different types of fleshing machine are available. One is a small game/bird flesher, which utilizes a wire wheel attached directly to a small electric motor, usually less than one horsepower. The mechanics are similar to the brush side of a bench grinder, except that the small game flesher incorporates side shields. These shields protect the taxidermist—and his work area—from any loose flesh particles. The wire wheel may be the easiest machine for beginners to learn on.

The second type of fleshing machine is called a rotary knife. It uses a round metal disc (most discs or blades are ten to fifteen inches in diameter) that has been sharpened around the edge. Instead of leaving the blade flat, the outermost eighth of an inch along the entire circumference is bent to form a 90-degree angle. This allows the user to pull the skin from left to right across the blade as it turns, removing any excess tissue. The rotary fleshing machine is generally better suited for critters larger than coyotes, but if used properly it can be effective on even the smallest mammals.

The type of fleshing machine you choose will depend on the type of work you plan to do. If you are embarking on a serious career in taxidermy, purchase both. But either kind of flesher will likely be the largest investment you'll make during the initial stages. Once the investment is made, though, either flesher will quickly pay for itself in the reduced time it takes to properly flesh a skin.

A wire-wheel flesher usually starts around $150 and a rotary-blade flesher upwards of $700. Fortunately, in recent years, Van Dyke's Taxidermy Supply has introduced what it calls the Dakota IV Detail Flesher. It is smaller in size than most commercial fleshers, but the cost is under $500. The Dakota IV may be a bit easier for beginners to work with than other rotary-blade fleshers because the blade and motor are smaller. Also, the blade on the Dakota IV turns at a much slower rate than those on full-sized fleshers.

Wire-wheel flesher.

Beginners who aren't sure if they'll like taxidermy can consider fleshing machines optional, as the fleshing can certainly be done—albeit slowly—with a standard knife and scissors. But I consider both wire-wheel and rotary-knife models high on the must-have list.

Tumbler. This is one of the highest-priced tools on the supply list and the only truly optional one in my mind. Don't interpret optional as not needed, though. A tumbler is a definite asset, although the art of taxidermy can be performed without one. The tumbler is a time-saver. Wet skins can be deposited in a tumbler and, after a short cycle, come out virtually dry, with only a slight touch-up necessary before continuing the mounting process. The action of the tumbler also helps reduce unwanted oils and enhances the hair's luster.

You can also add things like corncob grit or hardwood sawdust to the tumbler to aid in the cleaning and drying process. Corncob grit comes in two sizes, coarse and fine. Which you use is solely a matter of personal preference. It seems that most taxidermists prefer the coarse grit for mammal work, but some choose the fine, as well. The tumbler is filled one-third to almost half full with this tumbling

Rotary-knife fleshing machine.

mix. Many taxidermists like to add other ingredients to their corn-cob grit or hardwood sawdust to enhance performance. Two of the most popular additives include odorless mineral spirits and dry preservative, or both.

There are still taxidermists with years of experience who choose not to tumble their skins. They feel it creates as much work as it saves (e.g., removing tumbling material from hair and feet) and claim that the small amount of heat generated can be detrimental to a skin, particularly one that hasn't been tanned properly.

If used correctly, though, tumblers work well for cleaning and drying most mammal skins. So if you plan to make a longtime hobby or career of taxidermy, the tumbler will be a good investment.

Degreaser. To assure a quality long-lasting mount it is very important that you degrease the skin properly, particularly when dealing with fatty animals. This step can mean the difference between a good-looking mount that you will cherish for many years and one that starts off poorly and deteriorates quickly. You can find clear examples of poor fleshing and degreasing in older duck mounts that have started to yellow. Ducks are probably the toughest bird to flesh properly and the grease that bleeds through is more noticeable in their colorful feathers.

Proper degreasing can be accomplished in several ways. Many top taxidermists in the country swear by Dawn dishwashing liquid, claiming that it's the only degreaser they use. I've tried Dawn alone in the past, but I now prefer to use it in conjunction with a commercial degreaser. With a commercial degreaser, my animals felt much cleaner, dried quicker, and were much more shiny.

This is a must-have for a quality mount.

Dry Preservative or Tan. Dry preservatives work well on small game; their primary purpose is to remove moisture and bug-proof the skin. Most beginners start with a dry preservative or 20 Mule Team Borax, which is available at most grocery stores.

Numerous tans are available through taxidermy suppliers, and they usually work well. You also have the option of using a commercial tannery. While anyone who wants to learn the taxidermy process should learn the tanning process, a quality commercial tannery is highly recommended for beginners. This is especially true when dealing with particularly greasy or dirty animals.

Liquid Preservative. While liquid preservative can be used to soak an area, it is most often injected into areas like the feet and ears. (This only applies to a dry-preserved skin, as no liquid preservative is necessary for a tanned skin.) One widely used, easy-to-make preservative is a 50/50 mix of denatured alcohol and water. The syringes used to inject liquid preservative can be obtained through most veterinary or taxidermy suppliers. Handle syringes with extreme caution.

Bondo. It may seem strange to include what is usually considered an automotive supply item here, but without Bondo the taxidermy world would be scrambling for an exact substitute. Bondo has a wide range of applications in the taxidermy shop. In addition to small game work, it can be used to repair a manikin, or to secure the base of a spread turkey tail, or for attaching artificial fish heads, or as a base for antlers on big game manikins—the list is endless.

Bondo is indespensable in the taxidermy workshop.

No special formula is necessary for Bondo; just pick up whatever is available at your local convenience store or automotive store.

Many manikins that are larger than raccoons will be cut in half before shipping to save space. After the manikins arrive they must be put back together with Bondo. For small game and predator work, bondo is a must.

Wire. Wire can be used to secure and properly position limbs, tails, and ears. For small game and predators, wire is primarily needed for the tail, although it's also used internally in all manikins. (Rods are sometimes used in place of wire for manikin limbs.) Wire can be used to help mend damaged manikins or manikins that have been intentionally altered, as well. As it's relatively inexpensive, I'd recommend starting out with a small portion of each gauge (from 8 to 16) until you decide which you prefer.

Wire is not optional.

Manikins. Many years ago, a taxidermist had to clean the skull of the specimen he intended to mount, then add clay to form the muscles around the head to give it the correct shape. Next, the body had to be formed. This was done by first making a wooden frame,

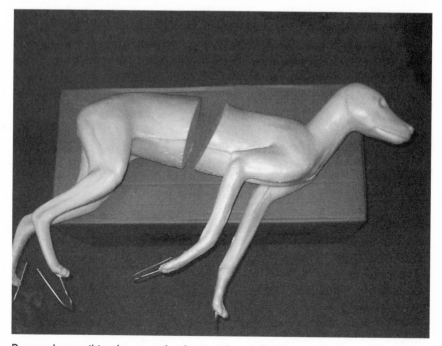

Pre-made manikins have made the taxidermist's job much easier. Most come with wires on the feet to attach the finished mount to a base.

and then adding excelsior to form the muscle groups. Once the taxidermist had a generic shape, he'd wrap twine around the mass to help hold it in place. These techniques were crude, of course, but they were the only methods available at the time.

Taxidermy evolved, as everything does, and top taxidermists around the country soon began a close study of various mammals. After casting, measuring, and studying thousands of specimens, they began to develop early models of the manikins available today. Modern manikins are made of hard foam that can be easily altered if the need arises, and they are highly detailed for a convincing appearance once the mount is complete. They can now be purchased in virtually every desirable position.

A quality manikin is mandatory.

Eyes. Put simply, eyes can make or break a mount. A mount can be beautiful in every other detail, but if a poor-grade eye is used the "alive" look that all taxidermists strive for just won't be there. On the flip side, an average mount with a high-quality eye can look great. Everyone seems to notice the eye first on a mount, so it's beneficial to install the best eye available.

The artificial eye has come a long way in the past twenty years. In the late seventies and early eighties most eyes looked like glass balls that had simply been cut in half. But today most eye companies produce at least one series of eyes that incorporates a correct shape (an eyeball isn't completely round) and true-to-life color. To produce the best work possible, make sure you use the highest quality eyes available.

Adhesive. Adhesive serves two purposes. It allows the skin to be moved about the manikin with little resistance, and once dry it will attach the skin firmly to the manikin, preventing it from "drumming." (This occurs when the skin dries and pulls away from any low spot on the manikin, thus forming a drum.)

Different types of adhesives are available. One of the oldest forms is a dextrin-based adhesive, which can take up to a couple of days to dry. This allows the taxidermist plenty of time to make last-minute adjustments. But, on the other hand, if the skin begins to dry and shrink before the adhesive dries properly it may drum. Many veteran taxidermists swear by a dextrin-based glue, and it definitely has a permanent place on most taxidermy shelves.

Epoxy is a relatively new adhesive for taxidermy. An epoxy adhesive consists of two parts that must be mixed thoroughly together before hardening occurs. Epoxy adhesives are useful because most will adhere and harden within two to three hours. This locks down the skin before it begins to dry, which helps alleviate any drumming. The drawback of using an epoxy, of course, is that the working time is much less than with other adhesives.

I recommend that beginners avoid an epoxy-based adhesive because mistakes are inevitable during the learning process and epoxy isn't very forgiving. After you gain experience, it will be easier to

Epoxy adhesive is a good choice for the advanced taxidermist.

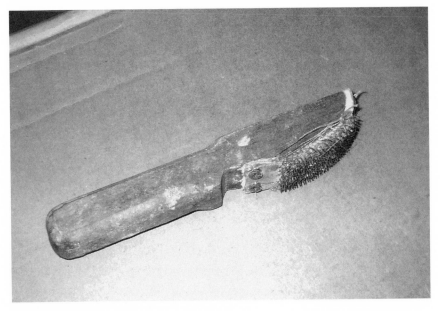

Stout Ruffer.

make the switch. A trick many taxidermists use is to apply epoxy to the facial areas, then use dextrin on the remainder of the body.

Adhesive is a definite must-have item.

Stout Ruffer. New manikins have a thin, slick layer on the surface that is impervious to adhesion. This is due to the release agent that is used to keep the manikin from sticking to the mold. To enable the skin to adhere to the manikin this outer layer must be removed. This is easiest done with a tool that roughens the surface of the manikin. A variety of tools will work, but many taxidermists prefer to use a Stout Ruffer, which simply scrapes the slick outer layer of foam from the manikin.

In addition to roughing a manikin, a Ruffer is very useful for positioning the skin during the mounting process. You'll definitely need some kind of Ruffer.

Thread. Thread is available in a wide variety of sizes and colors. The most popular color for taxidermy is black, but the determining factor will be the piece being sewn. A large dark animal such as a bear requires a heavy-duty black or brown thread. On the flip side, an albino squirrel requires a small-diameter light, or even white, thread.

Small-diameter thread is usually all you need to sew up small game seams.

Tail-Stripper. If you choose dry preservative, you'll have the option of slipping the tail instead of splitting it. If you decide to tan, however, the tail must be split. You can purchase a tail-stripper from any taxidermy supply house, but a pair of pliers or two screwdrivers also works well.

Regulator Needle. Regulator needles are very useful for positioning skins. They come in a variety of sizes, and everything from short to long seems to work fine. Regulators are inexpensive so you may want to buy several. They're optional, but very beneficial.

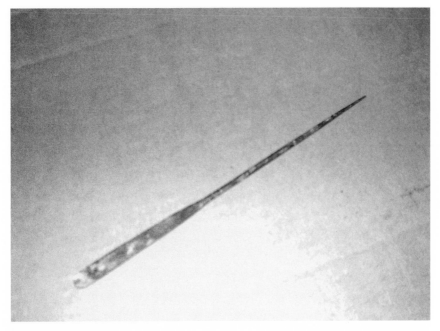

Regulator needle.

Airbrush. New airbrush techniques have allowed taxidermists to add the natural colors that really bring mounts to life. Not so long ago painting techniques were limited to what you could do with paintbrushes and automotive lacquers or oil paints. Highly skilled taxidermists could make do with these techniques, but it was tough on beginners. Those first attempts were often downright horrendous, leaving first-timers extremely frustrated with the results.

When the first taxidermists discovered the airbrush, probably around the 1980s, they were able to perform fantastic work. And around the time the airbrush was introduced to taxidermy there was also a giant leap forward in the paints being used. Instead of borrowing paints from other trades, someone began to formulate paints specifically for wildlife artistry. Experienced taxidermists can now produce an incredible finished product. And for beginners, it's possible to shave months—if not years—off the learning curve.

Many highly respected individuals in the taxidermy field remain devoted to the brush and oil paints, but their numbers are dwindling.

While the airbrush is optional, it is more than worth the investment required.

Airbrush and paint.

Air Compressor. If you buy an airbrush, you'll also need an air compressor. For beginners, the most basic style will usually be the best choice. Small portable tankless air compressors are available and work well if you plan on using them for nothing but the airbrush. But for other taxidermy needs I would recommend buying one with at least four horsepower and an eight-gallon tank.

Dremel Tool. A Dremel or similar tool with various bits is optional, but a very useful addition to your taxidermy equipment. You can use it to shape and prepare manikins, drill holes, and prepare your mounting base.

PUTTING IT ALL TOGETHER

Many supplies can be purchased through local vendors, but you will inevitably have to contact a taxidermy supply house, which is the only place to purchase much of the specialty equipment. (See Appendix for a full listing of major suppliers.)

An air compressor can be used to operate an airbrush or remove dirt and loose hair from a dried mount—among other things.

One of the oldest taxidermy suppliers in the country is Van Dyke's. They have helped taxidermists worldwide begin their hobbies or careers. They also have a vast assortment of virtually every type of taxidermy-related equipment. Van Dyke's even offers its customers technical advice from an on-staff taxidermist. This type of advice may be priceless if you find yourself stuck on a problem while right in the middle of mounting a hard-won trophy. To order a Van Dyke's catalog, call 1-800-843-3320, or visit their website at www.vandykestaxidermy.com.

3

Reference and Anatomy

I've always been amazed with the beauty of wildlife—and the art derived from such wildlife. It never mattered whether the artwork was photography, paintings, drawings, or taxidermy. But I was drawn to artwork, as it was actually re-created by the hand of man. At first, I thought there was some kind of secret or magic to drawing and taxidermy. How could someone know a deer, elk, or bear intimately enough to re-create it so perfectly? Then, during my first trip to Yellowstone National Park, I found a major part of my answer.

I had always wanted to visit this extraordinary place, so full of wildlife and majestic scenery. When I was finally able to make the trip, I spent the bulk of my mornings and evenings studying, photographing, and simply enjoying the abundant fauna. Midday, when many of the animals retreated into the forests to bed down, I visited some of the natural wonders. Inside one of the information centers I found an artist painting an exceptional portrait of a buffalo. I watched closely, trying to learn how he did it. I began to notice that the artist regularly peered through a small eyepiece on his workbench. I eventually asked him what he was looking at. He graciously offered, "Have a look."

Looking through the eyepiece, I could see a photograph of a life-sized buffalo identical to the one being painted. Somewhat confused, I asked why he was constantly checking the photo. He explained that all artists use reference material to duplicate anatomy, size, and other important features of their intended work. This cleared up a lot of unanswered questions for me. And this same rule of reference is just as important in taxidermy.

Without reference material our wildlife reproductions might more closely resemble cartoon characters than living creatures. The best wildlife artists in the world constantly study and observe the species they intend to re-create. This speaks volumes. Although a master taxidermist has competed in world taxidermy championships and probably mounted hundreds, if not thousands, of deer heads or small game, he will continue to constantly study his reference material for accurate reproductions.

Reference material usually takes the form of 2-D images, which include photographs and videos, and 3-D references, which include death masks and live specimens. All types of references are valuable when you're preparing to mount a species. And it is best not to rely on just one form.

One caveat, though. Don't use mounted animals as references. It is fine to study the work of another taxidermist; it's even recommended, as this may help with technique improvement. But a mount is an individual taxidermist's idea of what a creature should look like. No matter how well done, it won't be a perfectly accurate representation of a live animal, just that person's perception of the creature. Nothing can replace studying a live specimen and a variety of other reference materials.

To study a subject fully you must first obtain proper reference materials. These materials are probably one of the cheapest tools you can acquire. And they can usually be found right under your nose. If you want to mount your own small game or predators, or even deer, you are probably already a hunter. And almost every hunter I know has a few hunting videos lying around and stacks of hunting magazines that have accumulated through the years.

Studying photos of small game—like this beaver—in their natural habitat will help you create more realistic mounts.

Each month, these magazines are packed full of live photos of small game, predators, and big game. For the hunter and budding taxidermist they provide a double return on investment: You get all the good reading inside and also have the opportunity to study an endless array of wildlife photos. (And you have a great excuse when your spouse asks you why there are piles of hunting magazines all over the house.)

If you desire closer shots or more precise pictures, a full selection is available at most taxidermy suppliers. These photos include high-quality close-ups. The angles and positioning of ears, nose, eyes, and mouth are easily studied with these area-specific photos. I highly recommend getting at least one booklet from a qualified reference photographer, as well as acquiring all the other free photos you can.

An ideal way to begin a reference library is to buy several folders and label them with potential reference contents—one for squirrels, another for bobcats or raccoons, and so on. Once you're finished reading a hunting magazine, just sift through it and cut out the photos you need and keep them on file. This will give you a nice supply of poses and body positions to study again and again as needed.

Taxidermy suppliers often stock reference photos for a variety of small game.

Of course, the ultimate reference is a live animal. In a perfect world the taxidermist would have ready access to an animal pen or a pet for reference study. Most award-winning taxidermists consistently use live animals for reference. While some states allow the ownership of certain species of wildlife, do your homework before going this route. First, check state and local laws to find out if such ownership is legal in your area. Then learn as much about the animal and its care as possible. This will help head off potential problems related to feeding, environmental needs, and health care. Also, many of these wild creatures represent a hefty obligation. Bobcats, for example, can live nearly thirty years.

If you are just getting started, or if animal ownership is out of the question, other viable options remain. A collection of videos is great. Most hunting videos captivate their audiences by showing animals as they cautiously make their way to the hunter. Although most of these videos lean heavily toward big game (deer is probably the easiest to obtain), predator and small game footage is usually available. In a pinch, you can also visit a zoo or national park with a personal camcorder. The footage you collect this way may turn out to be invaluable. If your primary focus is squirrels, most city

Some species of small game are easier to keep as live reference than others.

parks are full of opportunities. And squirrels in a park environment will often come right up to you to beg for a handout, so it should be easy to get some quality close-ups.

Additional reference can be gained through your own hunting experiences. Once you familiarize yourself with what to look for it is amazing what you'll notice when watching wildlife.

I noted earlier that the death mask is a good 3-D reference. A death mask is a reproduction of a particular part of an animal's anatomy. For example, there are death masks for waterfowl skulls, big game noses and big game eyes (the entire area around the eyes), and even entire animal heads or facial features. These masks are made shortly after an animal's death, hence the name. A molding material (latex is popular, but other materials are available) is poured onto the body, then plaster is usually poured onto the latex to act as a "mother" mold. Once dry, the mold is cut in half and removed from the animal. After the mold has been rejoined, a material suitable for casting is poured into it. This forms a 3-D image with depth, distance, and angles that can't be studied with photos alone. As making these casts is a complicated procedure, I won't attempt to provide full instructions here. But commercial casts are available of almost any

It's a good idea to collect photos of every species possible; you never know when you'll get the chance to mount something a little different.

mountable animal. Also, videos and books devoted solely to molding and casting are available at most taxidermy suppliers.

After compiling enough reference material, you will be ready to start learning how to read and better understand this road map to a lifelike mount. To do this you must first understand how most people view a picture. If you show a picture of a bobcat grabbing prey to an individual untrained in reading reference and then ask him what he sees, he'll likely respond that he sees a bobcat. While this statement isn't wrong, it isn't the answer we're looking for. Ask the same question of someone trained to view and understand reference, and he will likely respond with comments about different leg angles, head, tail, and ear position, and so forth.

To do a competent job as a taxidermist you must break down a picture while studying it. Instead of looking at it as a whole, you must learn to notice each detail of your study piece. An excellent way to do this is to use straight lines within a photo to better understand angles and shapes that are pertinent to the re-creation of the subject.

Start by using a piece of paper with a small square cut out in the center. The size of the box will depend on the size of the photo you are working with. (The smaller the photo, the smaller the box.) Place the small box over a specific area of the photo that you want to study. For example, let's use the head area since that is one of the most prominent features in a life-sized mount. As you box off the eye, lay a ruler or any straightedge horizontally or vertically across the opening of the box. You will quickly pick up angles and shapes that were previously unnoticed.

When you start the actual mounting process, this will help you properly position the skin around the eye in a natural way. You will notice that the eye isn't round. Rather, it's an angled oval shape. Also, eye shape is heavily dictated by mood. A frightened or excited animal will have a wider eye, while the eye of a relaxed animal will be smaller, almost squinty, depending on the light level.

Another example might be to box off the ears of an alert bobcat and an aggressive one and then compare the two. You should immediately notice that the angle at which the ears flow into the head varies according to mood. By using the straightedge you will get a better understanding of how and where body parts should join for different poses.

Use the simple paper cutout to study photographs of every part of the animal you wish to mount; it's a wonderful tool for getting used to seeing what you need to see in order to create a lifelike pose.

As a taxidermist, your goal should always be to "perfectly" duplicate the specimen you are re-creating. This task is virtually impossible if you are not intimately familiar with the animal, which in this case happens to be small game or predators. As your experience grows, your ability to better understand and interpret references will only enhance your taxidermy skills. And learning how to study one specific animal will translate well when you move on to mounting other species.

ANATOMY

Anatomy, for our purpose, is the structure of a given animal. This includes the muscle and skeletal structure. You may think that anatomy is best left to the sculptors who spend countless hours reproducing manikins of the critter you want to mount. And it's certainly true that the bulk of the skeletal and muscular reproduction has already been completed for you with these manikins. However, who's to say the sculptor didn't make a mistake? They are human after all. Besides, learning as much as possible about a subject will always help you re-create it more naturally.

How would it look if we mounted a bobcat with a leg bent in the femur area, or with its ears sticking straight out from the sides of its head? It's funny to think about, but the finished product would be downright atrocious. While you might not make a mistake as obvious as those listed above, without a clear understanding of anatomy your mount will exhibit unnatural elements that are anatomically incorrect—however subtle. And if you need to make an alteration to the manikin you'll be using, things can get even trickier. So even though the manikin will do most of the anatomical work for you, it remains very important that the taxidermist learn as much as possible about his chosen subject.

When mounting big game, it's often easier to get away with a less-than-perfect understanding of anatomy. This is because the manikins produced for big game already include the body, neck, head, and legs (for a life-sized mount). You shouldn't allow this to dampen your enthusiasm for learning more about anatomy, though. And if you're working with small game manikins, you often won't have the luxury of pre-made pieces for shaping the extremities.

Anatomy isn't a subject that you can fully learn and understand after reading a few paragraphs or studying for a few hours. But if you get a good grasp of the basics, you will slowly accumulate knowledge about the subtleties of the species you study most often.

One way to learn more about anatomy is to pay close attention during the skinning process. Before any skinning takes place it is easy to swivel and bend an animal's legs, head, and other body parts to get an idea about range of motion. For example, you will be able to bend the leg of a coyote or bobcat only so far in any direction before a ligament or muscle group stops this movement. This will help you avoid overextending the leg in an unnatural position in the actual mount.

You should also notice how each bone is attached to the next while you're skinning an animal, and how the muscles attach and hold the bones. This is a never-ending learning process, as each animal has something new to reveal to you. It's one of the things that make taxidermy so fascinating.

By making mental notes of how all the parts go together you will quickly begin to understand what is natural and what isn't. And that is what taxidermy is all about: natural duplication.

CHAPTER 4

Skinning Methods

Proper skinning and fleshing are just as important as the mounting procedure itself. Although your trophy won't "come to life" until the actual mounting, without proper skinning and fleshing you'll never achieve the quality you're looking for. And the longevity of the mount will suffer.

Skinning procedures may seem difficult at first, but eventually they will become second nature. Until you are able to skin an animal with relative ease, it is best to practice as much as possible. Such practice is best performed on critters that aren't slated for mounting, because you're bound to make mistakes during the initial learning stages.

OBTAINING PROPER MEASUREMENTS

It is important to obtain and record some measurements both before and after the skinning process. These sets of measurements are helpful because it is best to put no more into the skin than is taken out. Some taxidermists rely on post-skinning measurements alone, but these can be misleading. To understand how this method can be skewed grab a dog gently by the skin on the back of the neck and give a lift; notice all the extra skin. Raw skin will stretch tremendously. To account for this, obtain a few measurements from the carcass—before skinning.

The eye-to-nose measurement should definitely be taken prior to skinning. This is best done using calipers, which are available at most taxidermy suppliers. To obtain an accurate measurement, place one tip of the calipers on the center of the nose, then open them until the remaining point rests in the corner of one eye. Then record the distance between the two points.

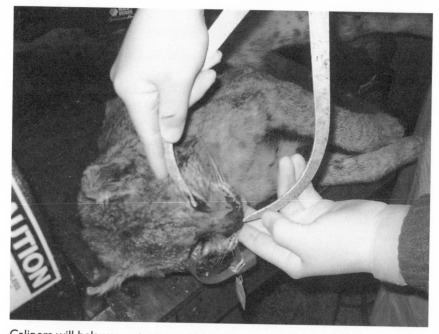

Calipers will help you get an accurate eye-to-nose measurement.

Measure from the nose to the base of the tail before skinning.

One other measurement should be taken before skinning: the length from the tip of the nose to the base of the tail. To obtain an accurate measurement, pose the animal how you plan to mount it. Then, starting at the tip of the nose, hold a flexible tape against the curvature of the body along the top of the skull and along the spine, extending it to the base of the tail or where the tail begins to protrude from the body. This should produce an accurate length measurement.

Other measurements can be taken after skinning is complete. The most important is girth, but neck girth and the length and width of the head are also useful. Girth should be measured after skinning because hair or fur can distort the measurement. Some taxidermists measure the girth prior to skinning and then subtract a small amount from the total to get an estimate. This will usually get you close, but it isn't always exact.

If you purchase an animal for taxidermy purposes it may already be skinned, or even tanned. Sometimes these skins will be accompanied by measurements; other times the purchaser isn't so lucky. When a carcass isn't available the taxidermist has to rely on skin measurements, estimations, and experience.

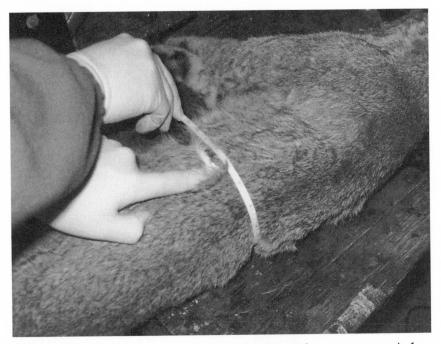

Although some taxidermists prefer to take the girth measurement before skinning, it's more accurate to measure after skinning.

To measure a skin without the carcass, spread it out evenly and uniformly, but don't stretch it. When you compare your skin-only measurements to a supply catalog, you may find that your recorded length is two inches too long while the girth is an inch too short. This is where experience is helpful. The skin might have been stretched a little in length, which would shorten the girth measurement. There isn't much you can do except order the closest possible manikin and begin test fitting.

Most taxidermy suppliers use the same measurements when describing their manikins. These include an eye-to-nose measurement, a length measurement (this is from the base of the tail to the tip of the nose), and a girth measurement (measured at the largest point of the midsection). Some include a neck girth (measured around the neck) and a measurement from the front of the nose to the back of the head. Even if the supplier you're using doesn't include these extra measurements it is still a good idea to record them. They might help with a proper fit, and they'll come in handy if you need to make alterations to the manikin.

SKINNING

Once the proper measurements have been taken the skinning process can begin. The old adage "there is more than one way to skin a cat" certainly applies here. The pose you choose will heavily influence the skinning method. Probably the most popular way to get started is with the dorsal incision. This incision is without a doubt the best for life-sized critters, which is how most small game is mounted. And it's the one we'll use exclusively when we mount a few specific species later in the book.

The ventral incision, or rug cut, is the next most used skinning method. If you are planning for a finished rug, this method is the only one to consider. But for a life-sized mount a full rug cut is very time-consuming, as more sewing is required to close the incisions.

Other skinning methods can be used for a shoulder mount or a half-life-sized mount. These aren't commonly used for small game and predators, but they can be effective. And for those looking for something different, a bobcat or raccoon pedestal mount is unique and attractive.

The Dorsal Incision

The dorsal-incision method uses only one straight cut from the base of the tail along the backbone, or slightly off to one side, and up to the shoulder area. The skin will then be peeled off, much like a pair of coveralls is unzipped.

To begin the dorsal incision, place the animal on its chest and stomach, with both the front and rear legs spread. It is best to start at the tail and cut forward. Insert the blade of a knife or scalpel at the base of the tail or just slightly in front. Now cut smoothly—and as straight as possible—toward the shoulder area. If a noticeable hair pattern exists along the center of the back it might be best to slightly shift the cut to one side. Not much, just enough to stray from these patterns. If no hair patterns exist simply follow the spine.

After the initial incision is complete it is beneficial to make small corresponding cuts on each side of the incision. Make these cuts very small, almost unnoticeable, and spread them a couple of inches

After making the initial incision from the base of the tail to the area between the shoulders begin to work the skin loose on each side.

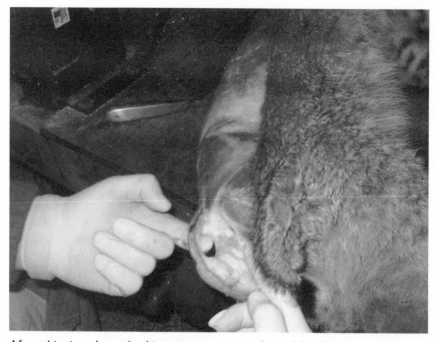

After skinning along the hips try to remove the tail by slipping it free, or if necessary split the tail on the underside.

apart. These marks will be used as reference points during the sewing process.

At this point, depending on the animal, most skins can be easily peeled from the carcass using only your hands. Grip one side at a time with your fingers and begin pulling the skin free of the body. It is usually best to begin along the midsection. When the skin has been pulled free as far as possible insert your hand between the skin and carcass and separate it further. Repeat this on the opposite side.

With the skin separated on both sides, begin working it free in the hip areas and down along the back legs. You should now have enough loose skin to pull it across the rear and downward, toward the feet. But first you will have to either cut the tail at the base or pull it free of the skin.

The method you choose for removing the tail section from the skin will depend greatly on the particular animal you're skinning and the preservation method. (See chapter 6 for a full discussion on preservation methods.) Stripping the tail works well for those who prefer dry preservative. The dry preservative can be applied with a piece of wire, which is used to carefully push preservative into the tail. This will leave you with no seams to sew.

The tails of raccoons, foxes, squirrels, and bobcats can be "slipped" rather easily. Hold the base of the tail at the point where it attaches to the body, and use a tail-stripper to pull the skin free from the flesh of the tail. You can fashion your own tail-stripper by using a pair of screwdrivers held together or by pinching a pair of pliers loosely around the tail section.

To slip the tail, simply wrap the stripper around the skinned portion of the tail, grip it at a point near the body, and give a firm, even pull. This may require some exertion, but the tail will eventually pop free.

Coyotes and groundhogs can be difficult if not impossible to slip, so the only alternative is to make an incision on the underside of the tail and skin conventionally. Be very careful when skinning a tail; the skin in this area can be very thin and is easily ripped. If the skin is going to be tanned (see chapter 6), splitting and skinning the tail is the only option, as this is the only effective way to ensure proper salt penetration.

Once the tail section is free of the skin, continue by pulling the skin toward the feet. Again, do as much of this as you can with your hands. If you reach a tight space, use a knife or scalpel to continue freeing the skin. Be careful to avoid cutting holes in the skin, though.

On most animals, the skin will separate easily down to the lower leg. Depending on the animal, relief cuts may then have to be made. Most bobcats, raccoons, badgers, squirrels, and groundhogs can be inverted all the way to the toes without these relief cuts. But for coyotes and foxes, they'll almost always have to be made. To make the cuts, start at the front of the big pad on the paw and cut up the back of the leg for six to eight inches.

Once these cuts have been made, or if the animal you're skinning doesn't require such cuts, continue freeing the skin downward on both legs. If the animal has dewclaws be sure to cut them free. When you reach the rear portion of the foot the skinning process will slow somewhat, and you'll need a scalpel to finish. Continue by pulling the skin with one hand while slowly working the scalpel around the foot until you reach the base of the toes.

At this point, some taxidermists cut the toes free and inject them with a liquid preservative, which often works fine. Others prefer to skin the toes entirely, all the way to the claw. Still others believe that it's fine to leave the last joint in the skin. I have cut the toes free and skinned them on occasion, although I wouldn't enter a taxidermy competition with a piece that had skinned toes. But for general work this method is fine. Also, keep in mind that if you plan to dry preserve a skin either method will be okay. But the toes should be skinned at least to the last joint if you plan to tan the skin.

Skinning the toes is very tedious, and in some cases it may take longer to skin all four feet than it does to skin the rest of the critter. Once you reach the base of the toes, try to get hold of the outermost toes, then slowly begin pulling them free of the skin. As the outermost toes are the shortest, they must be dealt with before the longer middle toes can be skinned. Slowly pull the toes free to the desired joint, and then separate. Do the same for the middle two toes.

Skinning is identical for all four feet. For squirrels, some taxidermists choose to sever the ankle or wrist joint and inject the entire foot with preservative. This seems to work fine, but I usually complete the skinning process to the base of the toes so only the toes themselves require injecting.

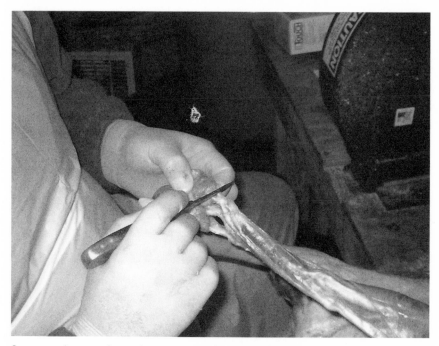

Separate the toes from the carcass at the desired joints.

After the skin is separated from the rear feet, pull it toward the front shoulder area. Once again, use a combination of pulling and careful cutting to loosen the skin. When you reach the shoulder area fold the front leg at what would be considered the elbow, and while pushing the front leg rearward, pull the skin forward. This will begin the skinning process on the front leg.

Continue pushing your hands between the skin and carcass forward of the shoulders. Once the skin is completely free around the elbow area, pull upward on the elbow while starting to pull the skin downward, toward the feet. Skin the front feet just as you did the back feet. After both front feet are skinned, the head and neck should be the only areas still attached to the carcass.

Now slowly pull the skin forward so that it separates to the rear of the skull. It will be necessary to use the scalpel to skin the head, so slow down and be careful not to cut through the skin. You should be able to completely skin the head by pulling gently and making small cuts to free it as you go along. The reason you need to be much more sensitive around the head is that it's always the focus of attention on a mount, and any cuts or damaged areas will be more easily noticed. Also, it's very important to leave certain tissues in the head area attached to the skin. These tissues aid in tucking and attaching the skin later on. Leaving these tissues will ensure the integrity of the surrounding visible areas, which include the eyes, ears, nose, and mouth or lips.

When you reach the rear of the skull, begin searching for the ear canal. While many taxidermists simply cut the ear free at the most convenient place, I prefer cutting it free deep within the canal. This will ensure anatomical correctness rather than leave you with an ear stuffed with clay.

To find the actual ear canal at the point where it enters the skull, begin by making several cuts into the muscle, slightly to the side and near the rear of the skull. If you don't find the ear canal simply move forward slightly and make another cut. As long as the cuts are being made into muscle tissue only, no harm is being done. Once the ear canals are severed, continue peeling the skin forward.

The skinning process slows again when you reach the eyes. If possible, insert a finger into the eye and pull the skin away from the skull. This will eliminate the possibility of cutting the eyelid. Slowly continue skinning. When you near the rear corner of the eye, make sure any necessary cuts are made very close to the skull. With the

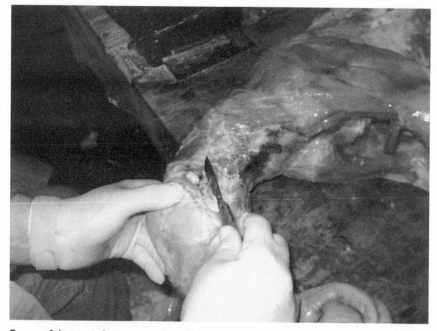

Be careful to cut the ear canal as close as possible to the point at which it enters the skull. This will make the rest of your work easier.

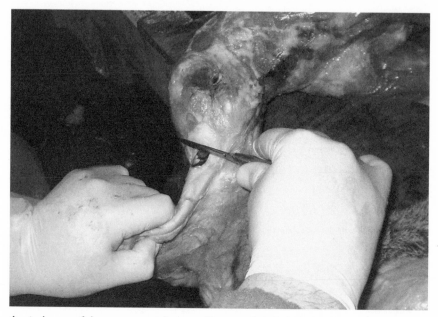

Again be careful as you near the eye. Cutting slightly behind the eye should help prevent any damage to the eyelid.

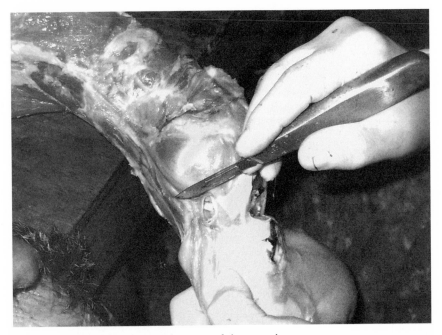

Begin cutting the skin free at the rear of the mouth.

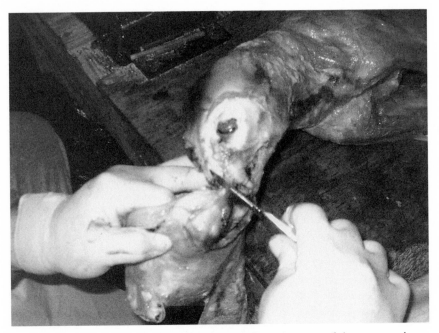

Be sure to sever the skin at least a quarter-inch to the rear of the nose pad.

rear corner finished—without damage to the eyelid—the remainder of the eye can be cut free from the skull.

After the skin is pulled forward of both eyes, it is time to concentrate on the rear corners of the mouth. Cutting the mouth free with plenty of lip skin will ensure that you can properly tuck the skin on a closed-mouth mount. It will also give you plenty of skin to tuck along the jaw on an open-mouthed mount.

First, use a finger to feel for the rear teeth through the exterior of the skin. Once you've located these teeth, begin cutting slightly behind them. Then, as an opening is made, insert one finger and pull the lip line away from the skull. As you skin forward—leaving plenty of lip line—it will be necessary to slow down to cut the skin free of the front of the mouth and to separate the nose area properly.

To cut the nose free, make an initial cut (depending on the size of the animal) at least an inch from the front of the nose. This is done on the skinned area as the skin is pulled forward of the head. This area should consist of cartilage and should be easy to cut. On smaller animals you may have to move toward the tip of the nose slightly to avoid cutting into bone. With the nose and front lip line severed, the skin should be completely free of the carcass.

Now you are ready to move on to fleshing and preserving your skin.

The Ventral Incision or Rug Cut

The ventral incision is made with a straight cut between the front legs from the anal opening to the chest area. Continue by cutting from each paw to the center of the body. Be careful to make the cuts as straight as possible if you're doing a rug cut.

If you choose to make a rug, it will be best to cut along the back of each leg, meeting at the anal opening. On the front legs, cut along the back of each leg until you reach the elbow area. Then angle very slightly toward the center of the inside of the leg, across the chest, with both cuts meeting at the abdominal incision. Finish the rest of the skinning process as you would with the dorsal incision.

Many taxidermists prefer to use only a short ventral cut, and this can be useful on small game. A short ventral incision includes only one cut from the anal opening to the center of the chest. Similar to a dorsal incision, but on the stomach/chest area rather than along the back, this method works great for hiding any stitching. It can cause

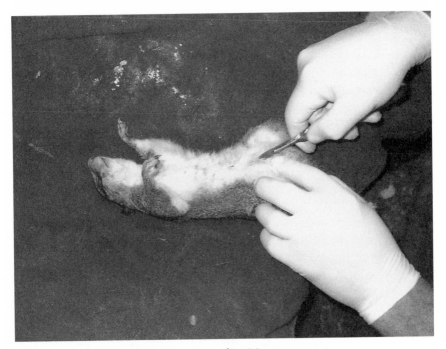

Some taxidermists prefer a short ventral incision.

problems for beginners, though, as the manikin limbs will have to be removed and reattached during the mounting process.

GUIDELINES FOR OPTIMUM SKINNING RESULTS

1. Leave as much flesh on the carcass as you can. This will make the fleshing process easier. Pulling the skin free as much as possible with your hands will help with this, as the skin should separate naturally from any muscle tissue. Cutting, although necessary in some areas, may leave you with a large amount of muscle tissue attached to the skin.

2. Avoid excessive cuts. This leads to extra sewing, which takes time and may reduce the quality of the finished product. Even careful, experienced taxidermists need to make cuts here and there. But as you gain experience, you'll learn to keep these cuts to a minimum. Recognizing the color changes along the line where skin meets muscle tissue will reduce the number of cuts you have to make.

3. Hurry, but take your time. Although this sounds contradictory, it actually works. It is obviously important to take your time while skinning because you'll avoid any excessive damage to the skin. On the other hand, it is very important to complete the skinning in as little time as possible to prevent slippage. The timeframe for slippage can be animal-specific, meaning some critters can take a lot more abuse than others.

   If you are a rank beginner, it might be best to start your taxidermy with more durable animals. Some of the easiest to work with are squirrels, groundhogs, and raccoons. I have found foxes and coyotes to be the most delicate. This is probably due to their scavenging nature, which may allow bacteria to gather around the facial area.

4. Make all incisions as straight as possible. Maintaining straight incisions and occasionally marking corresponding skin sides with small tic marks or holes will be very helpful during the sewing process. These marks will allow you to quickly match up both sides of the skin, letting hair patterns flow out evenly. Matching skin sides will also alleviate any binding that may occur if the skin is shifted from its original position.

5. Choose the skinning method that best fits the mount you've chosen. Ninety percent of all the life-sized mounts I complete are skinned with dorsal incisions. There are several reasons for this: the skin comes off nicely without any drastic bending or cutting of the carcass; less sewing is needed for this short incision along the back; and the seam along the back is much easier to reach and pull tight—meaning you don't have to sew between and along legs in areas that can often be tight.

   Sometimes, though, it is best to let the mount dictate the type of incision you choose. For a mount that will be lying on its stomach, it may be beneficial to do a short ventral incision. If you're making a rug, the rug cut is the only reasonable option. If the mount is for a competition or if you are extremely picky, hide the seam as much as possible. But if you're making a commercial mount, one that won't be critiqued by a judge, a dorsal incision will probably be fine—even for a mount lying on its stomach.

Fleshing

After the skinning process is complete it's time to flesh the skin. Proper fleshing includes removing all muscle tissue, thinning the skin slightly, and "splitting" or "turning" the face. Turning the face is the term used for separating the skin and tissues that surround the eyes, lips, and nose. In addition, the ears will be turned inside out so an ear liner can be inserted, which will make the ear rigid.

Use a scalpel or very sharp knife during the initial stages of turning and splitting the face. The general task of fleshing is best completed with a fleshing machine, which I highly recommend for any animal larger than a squirrel.

It will take some time to get used to a fleshing machine. My first experience with a flesher was on a deer cape. When I finished, hair was sticking through the inside of the skin and holes were plentiful—definitely not a professional job; the skin was actually beyond repair. But I learned a good lesson from that first attempt, and now my skins are top-notch. If possible, get used to the flesher by practicing on scraps of skin or on disposable skins, as mistakes are part of the learning curve.

A fleshing machine is also known as a "rotary knife" because the most common type incorporates a round metal disc that has been sharpened along the edge. The outermost portion, about a quarter-inch, is then angled to about seventy-five degrees. The blade is attached to an electric motor by a pulley, which rapidly turns the blade, creating a rotary knife. All rotary blades come with blade guards attached. It is important that these guards be left in place to prevent serious cuts to your hand and forearm.

CHOOSING A FLESHING MACHINE

Machines vary in quality as well as price, and beginners probably don't need to start with the best commercial fleshers. Most high-end commercial machines have strong motors that turn blades at higher-than-average RPMs. These machines enable taxidermists to produce a large amount of work in a short amount of time. But in the hands of a neophyte, such a machine will make a terrible mess.

For beginners, I would highly recommend the Dakota IV Detail Flesher from Van Dyke's Taxidermy Supply. This flesher was designed with the same quality standards as previous Dakota models, but the size has been significantly reduced. Along with a smaller motor comes a smaller blade, which turns at a much slower rate than larger machines. This detail flesher was designed for the small, tight areas that are prominent on the faces of larger game, such as deer, elk, and moose. But these machines are also ideal for small game because of the thinner skin you have to deal with. And if you are worried about purchasing a tool that will soon need to be upgraded as your skills improve, forget it. This smaller flesher is actually better suited to small game than many of the larger models. And it's also one of the most reasonably priced.

Another machine that is used by many small game and predator taxidermists is the small game/bird flesher. This flesher incorporates a wire wheel attached to a small electric motor. A wire wheel fleshes by pushing or stripping excess flesh from the skin. Although I prefer a rotary knife for most fleshing, certain jobs are ideal for the wire wheel, like working on the faces and legs of small critters. The wire wheel is also much easier for beginners to use. Even when it's used improperly, much less damage usually occurs than with a rotary knife. Also, if you branch out from small game to birds in your taxidermy work, the wire wheel will be nice to have around.

The only disadvantages for a wire wheel are that fleshing takes longer and the skin is left a little more ragged because the flesh is "wheeled" away rather than cleanly cut free.

ALTERNATIVES TO THE FLESHING MACHINE

Before the introduction of electric fleshers most taxidermists completed the fleshing process by hand. Today, nearly everyone uses a machine. But I do know a few professional taxidermists who choose to only hand flesh, and it's a good skill for a beginner to learn, as it gives you some versatility in your approach. Some taxidermists strictly hand flesh prior to the tanning stage, then use the machine during the shaving process, which is done after the initial pickling (see chapter 6). No set rule applies here, and as you find your own style you may realize that hand fleshing is all you need. And if you decide to use only dry preservative or send your skins to a commercial tannery, the need for a machine is further reduced.

One great advantage to hand fleshing is the minimal starting cost. A manufactured fleshing beam usually runs under $50, or you can simply build one yourself. With the purchase of a knife or tool specifically designed for fleshing—available at any taxidermy supply house—you'll have all the tools required to properly flesh most animals up to the size of deer. Hand fleshing also allows you to better control how much flesh is actually being removed.

The only disadvantage is that it requires much more time and yields results that are generally inferior to what a machine can do.

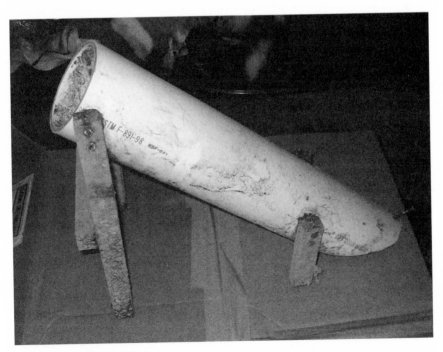

A homemade fleshing beam.

Building your own fleshing beam requires approximately a dozen 1½- to 2-inch wood screws, a 3-foot section of 4- to 6-inch diameter PVC pipe, and some wooden strips of various sizes. Cut one end of the pipe to an angle that allows for easy attachment to a tabletop. An approximate angle of forty-five degrees or less works fine, depending on personal preference. Start with a steeper angle, say sixty degrees or so, and position the beam on the table to see if it seems comfortable for fleshing. If not, adjust the angle slightly until you find something that works for you.

Some taxidermists like a steep beam, others prefer an angle that is nearly flat. Because these materials are inexpensive, you can always adjust the angle once you determine what best suits your needs. The end of the pipe that extends into the air can either be cut at a matching angle or left unaltered.

Once the pipe is angled correctly on the bench, attach wooden bracing on both sides. I use short lengths of 2×2 for this. The length of these braces will vary, as every beam is built to suit a specific user. A good starting length is around eighteen inches or so. Once the wooden legs are attached, drill a hole into the angled end of the pipe, which will be attached directly to the bench. Insert a wood screw through the pre-drilled hole and tighten it to the bench. This will prevent the beam from sliding around as you flesh the skin. That's all there is to it.

You may also want to have a small wooden fleshing beam that comes to a blunt point on the working end. To make this smaller beam, cut a 1×2 strip to around a foot or slightly longer. Angle the working end slightly so that it comes to a blunt point, small enough to stick into the eye of a bobcat. Sand thoroughly to ensure that all sharp edges, splinters, and raised knots are removed. Then attach the square end to a workbench with a wood screw. This beam will be used primarily to hand flesh small areas such as the face and legs.

TURNING THE EARS AND SPLITTING THE EYES, EARS, AND NOSE

I generally turn the ears and split the eyes, ears, and nose prior to the regular fleshing process, although this isn't mandatory. I like this method because once the face is turned I can concentrate fully on fleshing instead of having to stop to deal with the head.

The process of turning and splitting the face is very delicate work. The tissues surrounding the key areas are very thin, so it's important to proceed slowly. I prefer a scalpel for this work, as few knifes can be sharpened well enough to cut without having to be pushed slightly.

I usually start the splitting process at the lips and nose and then work back. Hold the lip between your thumb and fingers and begin to split it. Do this by cutting very slowly between the skin and the tissue that is basically doubled back onto it. The scalpel will separate the tissues so the lips can lie perfectly flat.

Continue around the lip line until it is completely separated. You will quickly acquire a feel for what is correct. The skin will feel flat and flowing, instead of lumpy, which occurs when an area isn't split all the way. With the lip line complete, it's time to start working on the nose.

While all facial areas are important, the nose is one of the more prominent features—a real eye-catcher. When you look at a mount, you probably notice the eyes first, with the nose a close second. I have seen mounts that were put together well except for the nose, which basically ruined them. If you look closely at a poorly constructed nose you may see large waves or bumps. This is due to improper turning and fleshing. The more flesh left attached to the skin, the more shrinkage can occur. So it is very important to split the nose thoroughly and flesh it as thin as possible.

To begin, lay the nose flat on the end of your index finger. Cut carefully through the center with a scalpel. The nose is made of cartilage, but this should pose no problems. Go slowly to prevent cutting the outside of the nose pad. You will quickly learn how to feel for thickness with your fingers and how close you are cutting to the surface of the skin. Make the cut as close to the center as possible.

Next, begin to separate the surrounding cartilage from the skin itself. Again, if you go slowly you should have no trouble. But there is one area that can be tougher than the rest. The wings of the nose, because of the way they're shaped, are usually the toughest areas to thoroughly split.

Now turn your attention to the eyes. Place an index finger through the eye opening and begin separating the membrane along the eyelid. (If the eye is too small, as with a squirrel, insert your finger through the mouth and lay the eye on the tip of your finger, then work around the entire area.) Use the scalpel to separate the lid all

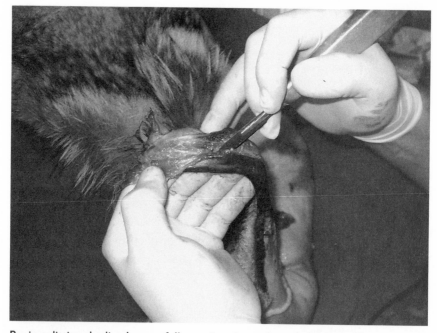

Begin splitting the lips by carefully cutting above the overlapping skin.

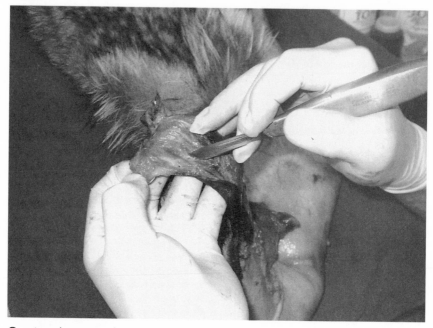

Continue by cutting between each skin layer.

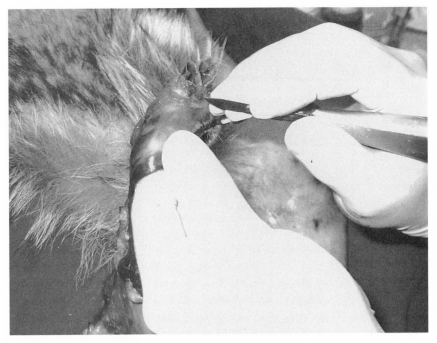

Cut slowly around the outer edge of the nose.

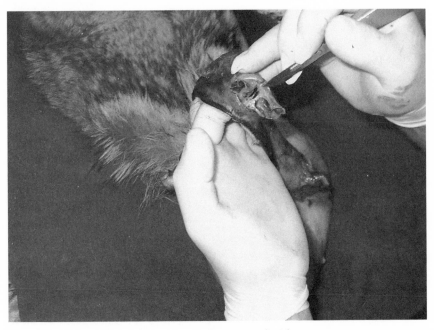

Cut along the center of the nose to separate each side.

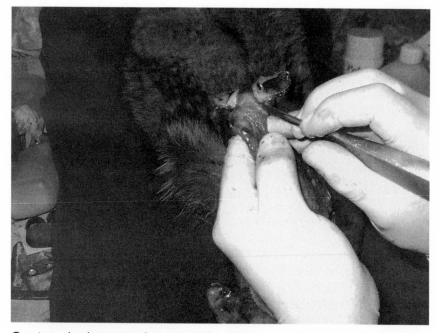

Continue slowly turning the nose to the outermost area.

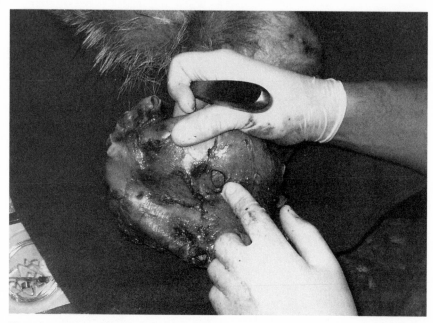

Turn the eye by inserting a finger into the eye hole, then work slowly to prevent damage.

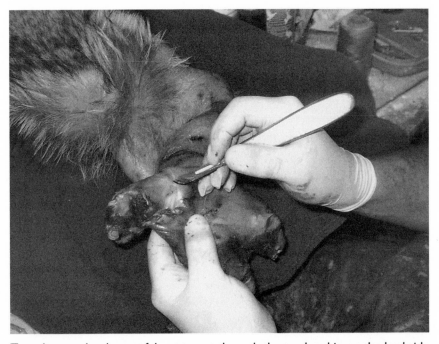

Turn the ears, but be careful not to cut through the tender skin on the backside of the ear.

the way to a fatty membrane located on the very edge of the eyelid. If this fatty tissue is not removed, more shrinkage than normal will take place. After splitting both eyelids, move on to the ears.

To turn the ears properly, separate the muscle tissue at the base of the ear from the surrounding skin. Then use a finger and the scalpel to gradually separate the skin to the tip of the ear. This is the most common method and one that must be used for coyotes and larger game. For working with bobcats and animals with smaller ears, I picked up a valuable technique from wildlife sculptor and award-winning taxidermist Tab Hinton. His method involves first separating the ear nearly a third of the way. Stop the turning at this point and remove the remaining muscle tissue surrounding the ear butt. Then, during the mounting process, fill the turned portion of ear with a small amount of clay and inject the unturned section with liquid preservative. This method is very effective, and it's normally how I deal with the ears of smaller game. (This method will be discussed further in chapter 8.)

Once the entire face is split you can get on with fleshing the body, legs, and face. No matter what method you choose for fleshing—rotary knife or by hand—I recommend fleshing from the tail forward. This is a must for certain animals, so you might as well get into the habit of doing all skins this way.

FLESHING WITH A ROTARY KNIFE

Fleshing with a rotary knife is the fastest way to complete the bulk of the job. Once you're familiar with using a rotary knife, you'll be able to thin and flesh even the thinnest of skins in short order. But until then, just go slowly. If you purchase a new machine, a video detailing proper fleshing methods may be included. If not, I'd suggest buying one.

For small game and predators, you may want to use the machine primarily on the body. When you're just starting out it's often easier to hand flesh the remainder of the skin, face, and legs on a beam. Once you've gained some expertise, you may be able to flesh these small areas on the machine, as well.

To begin, grip the area at the base of the tail in your right hand (most fleshing machines work from left to right), and hold the forward portion of skin in your left hand. While you're still in the learning stages, it will be best to spread your hands only eight to ten inches apart. As you gain confidence, you may want to widen your grip, but early on a narrow grip allows you to work slowly on one small section at a time. Also, if you happen to go through the skin, the cut should be small.

Slowly pull the skin from left to right and you will see any attached muscle tissue begin to peel off. Most small game and predators, because of their small size, have very thin skin, especially when compared to big game. For this reason, you should try to just skim the surface by adjusting the guards and the angle of the blade to a very shallow bite (instructions for this should accompany any model you buy). The tracks made by a rotary knife are very easy to see, so once an area is free of flesh, move your grip slightly to start on a new area. Flesh the entire body area up to the neck.

To finish fleshing the legs, it is best to use the small wooden beam described earlier. Slide the dulled point of the beam into each leg as far as possible without damaging the skin. Then slowly and lightly cut away any remaining flesh. I'd recommend a knife for this, as a scalpel can be too sharp for these thin areas. If only a small

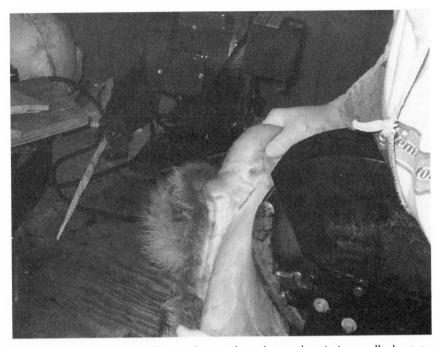

Fleshing with a rotary knife can be quick and easy, but it is usually best to complete the face by hand.

amount of muscle tissue is attached to the leg area you may want to just skip the fleshing in this delicate area. Also, if you're using dry preservative, you may be able to pull off any small amounts of tissue left after the powder is applied.

The last area I flesh is usually the face. Even for experienced taxidermists, it often pays to flesh the faces of small animals by hand. The face is probably the most delicate area that you'll work with. Mistakes are tougher to cover up, and the skin is generally thinner in this area.

Begin by sliding the head onto the wooden fleshing beam. Then position the lip onto the end closest to you. For fleshing these thin areas I have gotten comfortable with using a scalpel, but a beginner may want to use a skife knife, which is a razor blade with a guard attached (available through normal taxidermy suppliers). A knife is yet another option although, as I stated earlier, I can't get a knife sharp enough to suit me. If you are just starting out, I'd recommend a skife knife.

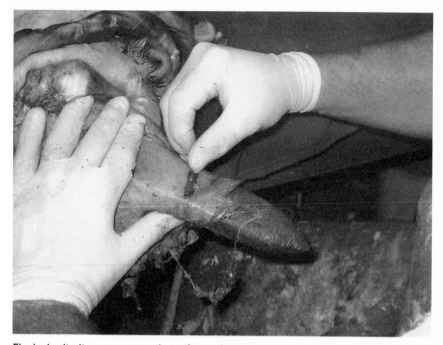

Flesh the lip line to a smooth, uniform shape.

Now slowly begin to flesh the lip area until only very thin skin remains. Rotate the lip line slightly, then repeat. Do this until the entire length of the lip line is properly fleshed. Now move on to the nose.

Attempt to insert the end of the beam into each nostril. If this can't be done you may have to use the end of an ink pen housing. Regardless of what you improvise, make certain it is free of lumps. A smooth surface is important because lumps may cause you to cut a hole in the skin during the fleshing process. Once you have something firmly in place, slowly shave the surrounding area until it is thin and free of flesh.

After the nose is complete, pull the skin onto the beam until the eyelid surrounds the end of the beam. I can't stress enough that all facial areas are very thin and easily damaged, and the eye area may be the most vulnerable of all.

Using your chosen blade, cut slowly toward the eye. You should see a row of fat within the eyelid. This fat is at the very tip of the eyelid and is white in color. To thoroughly flesh the eye, you'll have to carefully remove this fat. Continue fleshing around the eyelid.

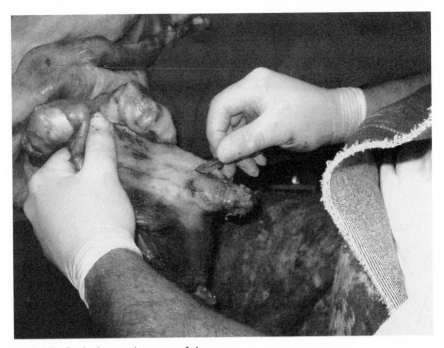

Carefully flesh the tender area of the eye.

Once both eyelids are properly fleshed, begin to slowly rotate the face using the eye as a center point locked onto the beam. As you are rotating the face, carefully cut free any remaining flesh. The flesh between the eye and nose, eye and opposite eye, and eye and rear jaw all needs to be removed.

Then place the lower jaw on the beam and remove any excess flesh there. Also, I like to thin some in the whisker area (but not too much). If you remove too much flesh from this area the whiskers may fall out.

When you finish with these areas, give the skin the once-over, using a small pair of scissors to snip free any remaining flesh.

The fleshing process should now be complete and the skin ready to either dry preserve and mount or salt and prepare for the tanning process. If you are going to use the dry preservative method I would recommend that you get the skin as flesh-free as possible.

If you're going to tan the skin, small amounts of flesh can be left for now. This excess can be removed later during the tanning process. Also, the skin will usually be thinned during the pickling stage of tanning, so that the pickle fully saturates the skin. But I believe that most small game skins are so thin that this step is optional. (See chapter 6 for more details on this process.)

If you do choose to shave further after pickling, you'll drain the skin, then continue with the same procedures just described for fleshing. You'll be able to remove any tissue that was left, but the primary goal of shaving after the pickle is to thin the skin, so be very careful.

USING A WIRE WHEEL

The instructions for using a wire wheel are very similar to those for using a rotary-knife flesher, although you'll be dragging the flesh from the skin instead of cutting it free. Remember not to get any one area too hot while using the wire wheel. This may occur if an area is held under the pressure of the wire wheel for any length of time. The heat is caused by friction, so just keep the skin moving.

One advantage that I've found when using the brush is that I'm able to flesh almost the entire skin without using a knife. However, you'll still need to hand flesh around the eyes, lips, and nose. The remainder of the face can be fleshed with the wheel. While it's possible to use stiffer wire, I'd recommend that you use a soft wire wheel while learning.

BEAM FLESHING

We've already discussed the relative merits of using a fleshing machine, and hand fleshing, but for an animal as small as a squirrel you should probably do all the work on a fleshing beam.

Lay the skin on the larger beam you've affixed to the top of your workbench. Place the skin with the head facing down toward the bench. Allow the tail and rear legs to dangle from the uppermost point of the beam. Now lean lightly into the rear of the beam, which should help you hold the skin in place.

Using a knife or fleshing tool, begin to slowly cut any flesh free from the skin as you apply pressure toward the table. When you finish with an area, rotate the skin slightly and continue until all the flesh is removed. Next, pull the skin toward your chest and continue removing flesh along the stomach, chest, and back areas.

Once this has been completed, continue hand fleshing the legs and face as discussed earlier.

Always remember to make sure that the skin lies flat on the fleshing beam and that no lumps exist—things like cockleburs, mud clods, or other contaminants. Lumps between the skin and fleshing beam may cause you to cut holes in the skin, which you want to avoid at all costs.

CHAPTER

Preserving Your Trophy

Preserving the skin of your trophy before mounting will allow
you to enjoy your work of art for as long as possible, hopefully a lifetime. And this includes your first mount. Even as your
skills progress, and I can assure you that they will if you devote time
to the art, you will enjoy looking back on your first few attempts.
Not only at the trophy you collected, but also the improvements you
made along the way.

If your interest in taxidermy lasts longer than a few minutes, you
will be sucked into the controversy surrounding preservation methods. The debate centers on dry preservative versus a true tan, and
there really is no right answer.

I actually support both methods—but only to a certain extent. For
instance, I would never tan a squirrel. I just don't think there's any
need to, but there are many taxidermists who insist on tanning a
squirrel. Conversely, I would never dry preserve a moose or a bear,
but there are some who would. Both methods have a secure place
in the world of taxidermy.

In my own taxidermy operation I use dry preservative, in-house
tan, and occasionally send skins to a commercial tannery for larger
projects or when time is short. The decision for when to use which
method depends on a variety of factors, such as the type of animal
being mounted, time constraints, and so on.

Most advocates of dry preservative note that it is quick and reli-
able and that the results are excellent. Many respected taxidermists
around the country use this method exclusively. And they put out
quality work, better than some others who abide by a strict "tan everything" rule. In fact, a friend of mine who competes regularly in world
competitions uses dry preservative on occasion, although he primarily
tans his skins. He consistently earns ribbons, and has done so using
dry preservative.

Other taxidermists, of course, swear that tanning is the only way to achieve quality results. They insist tanning is the only method to use for competition or commercial work. All advocates of this method argue that tanning is a much more effective method of preservation, with a longer product life, and easier to work with. Frankly, most dedicated competitors use only tanned skins, but, as I noted earlier, there are certainly exceptions.

Complete tanning involves several steps: salting, pickling, and a final tanning soak or brush-on tan. There are also modern variations that simply involve a soak in a tanning solution, although diehard tanning advocates claim this is no better than using a dry preservative. There are an abundance of tans available, and we'll take a closer look at these later in this chapter.

Dry preservative, on the other hand, consists of only one step: a dry preservative application following a thorough fleshing. This makes the work a lot quicker, as the taxidermist can skin, flesh, wash, preserve, and mount all in one day. Dry preservatives do vary in quality, though. Most companies offer dry preservatives that are recipe specific, and different companies prefer different dry preservative recipes.

Competition-quality mounts are usually tanned, but dry preservative works just fine for most small game.

If you ask around, you'll quickly find that taxidermists—hobbyists or full-timers—each use a variation of one of the two major preservation methods that has proven compatible with their individual styles. After some experimentation, you will eventually reach this point, too.

Let's start with a look at the basics of each approach.

DRY PRESERVATIVE

Dry preservative is a powdered chemical substance that, if applied properly, will preserve and protect the skin from bacteria growth. Most dry preservatives are a mix of chemicals that discourage bugs from infesting the specimen and help eliminate odors. Moths, in particular, can be detrimental to a mount. So a bug deterrent is an advantage in dry preservative. But many taxidermists claim this bug-proofing will eventually dissipate, leaving the trophy vulnerable to infestation. All I can say is that none of the veteran taxidermists that I know who use dry preservative regularly have had any problems with bugs (including me).

As with any organic product, if conditions are made ideal for bugs, they'll eventually become a problem. To avoid damage, regularly monitor your mounts and take appropriate action to maintain an environment conducive to their longevity.

Although some taxidermists call any powdered preservative a "quick tan," no stabilization of the structural proteins within the skin takes place when using dry preservative, which means that it shouldn't be considered a tan.

A dry-preserved skin is essentially rawhide that has had the moisture removed. It can return to a raw state at any time if enough moisture contaminates the skin. But the moisture content in the air would have to be extremely high for a very long time for a skin to return to such a state. Incidentally, the same high level of moisture could have a harmful effect on a tanned skin too, although it would not return it to rawhide.

Because skin has a moisture content of approximately sixty to seventy percent, it would quickly be destroyed by bacteria if left unpreserved. Remember that during field care moisture and warmth combine to promote bacteria growth. To help eliminate moisture in the skin, dry preservative relies heavily on desiccants.

Desiccants are chemical drying agents that absorb and help prevent the reoccurrence of moisture in the skin. This is why dry preservative is so named: It preserves with a drying action. Bacteria, which break down the epidermis, can't exist in a moisture-free environment, so no deterioration takes place.

A second major ingredient in a dry preservative is a surfactant. Surfactants aid in the absorption of the desiccant. They help the preservative better penetrate the skin. Scientifically speaking, the surfactant lowers the surface tension of the moisture in the skin. This counters the skin's natural tendency to repel foreign substances and allows the skin to absorb the preservative.

There are some things you can do to help alleviate problems associated with the dry-preservative method. Start by allowing whatever dry preservative you choose to thoroughly penetrate. It is sometimes best to apply the preservative heavily, then fold up the skin and lay it on a towel in a refrigerated or cool area. Let it stay there overnight before shaking the excess free and reapplying.

Once the mount is completed, keep it in a controlled environment. Ideal conditions are between sixty and eighty degrees, with low humidity. (This is also true for tanned products.)

Because significant shrinkage does occur with dry preservative, it's a good idea to use a high-quality hide paste. Epoxy adhesive is considered one step above regular hide paste, and I highly recommend it any time you use dry preservative. The epoxy locks down the skin before it has time to dry and shrink. More shrinkage will occur with a generic hide paste.

Criticism of dry preservative has often come from taxidermists who didn't take proper precautions before using it. Perhaps they didn't flesh the skin properly or take accurate measurements of the animal being mounted. These are the two most common problems among dry preservative users. What every taxidermist must understand is that a flesh-covered, thick-skinned area will shrink considerably more than a well-fleshed, thin-skinned area. Also, a raw skin can be stretched considerably more than a tanned one.

While both tanned and dry-preserved skins will shrink during the drying process, the majority of the shrinkage in a tanned skin has already taken place during the tanning process. In a dry-preserved skin, however, all shrinkage occurs after mounting. So with dry preservative, it's imperative that you get exact measurements of the carcass and flesh the skin thoroughly. If you pay attention to these early procedures, you should be able to achieve good results with dry preservative.

TANNING

Learning the chemical composition changes that take place within a skin during the tanning process may help you decide whether you'd like to use this method. Taxidermists who choose the tanning system usually do so because they like the fact that the skin is more stable during the mounting process (less shrinkage) than with dry preservative.

To understand this stability you must first know what skin is actually composed of. Skin is a mixture of moisture and proteins. And some proteins are soluble and some insoluble. I once read a very accurate description of skin composition in a "breakthrough" taxidermy manual. The manual stated that a good analogy would be to think of a skin as a leafy tree. The trunk and limbs represent the structural, or insoluble, proteins. The leaves represent the blood, fats, and soluble proteins.

To stabilize a skin you must first remove these leaves, leaving only the limbs. But you can't stop at this stage or your tree limbs will eventually collapse because nothing is cushioning them. Basically, this means that when dry preservative is used the bulk of the soluble proteins are pulled from the skin but replaced with, well, nothing. This is why a bit more shrinkage occurs in a dry-preserved skin.

When tanning is completed properly, though, the leaves (soluble proteins) are replaced with tannins. Tannins can be thought of as artificial leaves. These act as fillers that attach themselves to the skeletal, or insoluble, structure. These tannins also help lubricate the structure, preventing it from eventually collapsing and becoming glued together. This means you're left with less shrinkage and a more stable product—at least in theory.

Complete tanning encompasses up to three steps, although in recent years new methods have been developed that provide shortcuts around the full process. For the normal tanning procedure, any missed steps leave a skin less stable.

If you choose to conventionally tan a skin, start by applying a medium layer of salt once the skin has been properly fleshed and the eyes, lips, nose, and ears turned. The salt extracts the soluble proteins—blood, fats, and oils—from the skin. Once the salt is applied and rubbed into every area, roll or fold up the skin with all cuts and openings to one side, so adequate drainage can take place. Then set it aside, preferably at a gentle angle with the openings on the low side. Placing the skin on an upside-down milk crate also works well, as fluids can drain away without pooling. After twenty-four hours, unroll the skin and shake free any excess salt. Repeat the salting procedure.

Once the second salting has taken place you may continue the tanning process, or store the skin in a dry environment until you are ready to continue. In high-humidity areas, it may be wise to place the skin in a freezer if you can't work on it right away. Even when I send a skin to a tannery, I like to open it and hang it in a breezy area or in front of a fan to further dry it and prohibit drainage during shipping.

After the salting stages are complete, again shake the excess salt from the skin. Continue by placing the skin into a salt solution with a ratio of 1½ cups of salt to 1 gallon of cold water. The amount of solution depends on the size and number of skins to be soaked. For one bobcat skin, start with about 1½ to 2 gallons of solution. Soak the skin for approximately thirty minutes.

This procedure is critical, as the salt solution will prevent the skin from acid swelling from the pickle solution in the next step. This soaking stage also helps the pickle penetrate flinted or thoroughly dried skins faster.

Once a dry skin returns to a soft state, you're ready to continue.

Place the skin into a pickle bath, which will further dissolve and remove the soluble proteins within the skin. The acid will also break up the natural bonds of the proteins and prepare the skin fibers to bond with the tannins that will be introduced in the tanning bath.

The pickle bath is a mixture of salt and acid. Several types of acid are available from taxidermy suppliers, and only experience can dictate which one you'll like best. I'd recommend "Safetee Acid" if you're just starting out. This is a relatively new acid that is less harmful to the user and the environment than many other acids. It will also maintain a low, steady pH level, which is helpful.

For mammal skins it is important that you maintain a pH level between 1.5 and 2.5, with 2.0 being ideal. Most acid comes with instructions on how to achieve the proper pH level. Soak time varies with the thickness of the skin and the pickle being used. A safe rule is to soak the skin in the pickle for twenty-four hours, then remove, flesh, and redeposit for an additional twenty-four hours.

Don't worry if you can't remove the skin from the pickle right away. I've left skins in the pickle solution for up to a couple of weeks with no problem. Just remember to check and regulate the pH if you let the skin go longer than two 24-hour periods. If the pH level rises above 3.0 you may experience problems.

Once the pickle soak has been completed the taxidermist must determine whether the skin being tanned should be degreased. While many animals require no degreasing, some do. Among small game, raccoons top the list. Among predators, coyotes will probably need to be degreased, depending on the individual skin. Sometimes it is also beneficial to degrease animals that are not known to have greasy skins. The degreaser helps to clean and shine the hair and eliminates any oils that may be contained in the skin. This step is optional for squirrels, bobcats, and many other animals, but a degreasing soak can help any skin looks its best.

Methods for degreasing vary slightly. Some taxidermists like to "neutralize" the skin before degreasing (raise the pH level to a neutral state). Others, myself included, choose to degrease while the skin is still in a pickled state. I like this approach because I think it heads off problems that may occur after the neutralizing process.

Raccoons usually need to be degreased before mounting, although this step can be bypassed for many other species of small game.

As with acids and tans, numerous degreasers are available. As I mentioned in chapter 2, some taxidermists use nothing but Dawn dishwashing liquid as a degreasing agent. While I also use Dawn, I like to use degreasers made specifically for degreasing skins, too. Most are effective if the directions are followed properly. An excellent degreaser to start with is Epo-Grip Bloodout/Degreaser HD.

Following the pickle and degreasing stages, you might want to neutralize the skin if you haven't already. Raising the pH level to a neutral state allows the skin to accept the tannins, which, in essence, are artificial proteins that cushion the skin structure and stabilize the skin so decay won't take place.

Begin by mixing two tablespoons of baking soda to each gallon of water. The pH level for the neutralizer should be around 7.0. If the pH is higher, just add water. If the pH is lower, add a small amount of baking soda, mix thoroughly, and recheck.

Now deposit the pickled skin into the neutralizer. You may have to add weight to the skin, as it will probably float. After a soak of between fifteen and twenty minutes, remove the skin and rinse immediately.

The last step is the actual tanning. One of the most popular in-shop tans in recent years has been Knobloch's Liqua-Tan, which I use as my primary tan. Simply apply Liqua-Tan to the entire flesh side of the skin. Next, you may roll the skin up and place it in a freezer to work on later (the tan will actually soak in while the skin is in the freezer) or let the skin sit for six to eight hours before continuing.

Once the skin has been allowed to soak up the tan, I place a small amount of Dawn dishwashing liquid into two gallons of water and quickly wash the skin. The tan will not wash out, but any excess oil will. Now rinse thoroughly and proceed with the mounting process.

COMMERCIAL TANNERIES

A quality commercial tannery can save you a lot of time and frustration. Notice I used the word "quality." Check with fellow taxidermists and you will quickly learn who these companies are. Granted, if you deal with a tannery long enough a problem will arise. But it is the frequency of the problems that you should be most concerned about. And remember, even quality tanneries can't fix every problem. Proper field care and prep work by the hunter and taxidermist are still very important.

For the beginner—or professional, for that matter—who wants to devote all his time to the mounting procedure, or for anyone who doesn't have the time or space for all that tanning requires, a commercial tannery is ideal. And if you're starting on your first taxidermy project, it will be much easier to work with a properly cleaned, tanned, and degreased skin. Working with a poorly preserved skin may frustrate you to the point of quitting, when all you really need is a better place from which to start.

The best tannery I have worked with is East Coast Tannery, which is located in Pennsylvania. I've never had a problem with them, and I highly recommend their service to newcomers. To contact East Coast Tannery, call 1-877-TAN-FURS, or 215-257-9479. They will be glad to provide instructions for shipping your skin.

Reading about all these choices may overwhelm you, but don't let it dampen your enthusiasm. After many years in the taxidermy business I have found that nothing is always right and nothing is always wrong. Advancements come from those willing to step out and try things that no one else will try. Learn the basics and then find methods that suit your style and the type of projects you work on.

I base a lot of my decisions about various procedures on the circumstances surrounding each trophy. Customers may want things done a certain way, or I may need to make adjustments to deal with how an animal was cared for in the field. No matter what method you settle on, do it well and you'll be happy with the results.

Using dry preservative is very easy, and I feel it is 100 percent effective on small, thin-skinned animals. So throughout the remainder of this book we will refer to this method because it is an excellent way for the beginner to get started. As you gain knowledge about taxidermy, you may want to switch to the tanning method. Or you may choose to start with a commercially tanned skin.

CHAPTER

7

Mounting a Squirrel

Most aspiring taxidermists will work on whatever animal they can obtain. One young lady, who has built somewhat of a reputation among fellow taxidermists in the Southeast for being devoted and very resourceful, actually began by mounting road-kill that wasn't mangled beyond repair. It may sound strange, but I actually mounted a moose before ever mounting a squirrel, although squirrels are great animals for budding taxidermists. It's also worth noting that mounting a squirrel isn't much different, in method any-way, from mounting a life-sized bear. Bears and other big game are simply much bigger, requiring more sewing and more costly materials.

Squirrels are easily to obtain, and they actually lend themselves well to the mounting process. A very tough skin and a better-than-average resistance to slippage places them at the top of the begin-ner's list. The only disadvantage to mounting a squirrels is that its small size obviously creates some tedious detail work. On the other hand, if you learn to deal with these small details now it may help when the time comes to work on larger critters.

Squirrels make a great addition to almost any game room or tro-phy display. And collecting the different types of squirrels is a lot of fun. The gray squirrel is easily the most popular. It can be found throughout the East and over a large portion of the remainder of the country.

I stick with dry preservative for squirrels because their tough, thin skin is ideal for this method. And it's convenient to use dry preserv-ative on your first project. I'd rather see beginners concentrate on proper skinning, fleshing, and mounting than get involved in the de-bate over preservation methods.

Because the materials for mounting a squirrel are relatively cheap in comparison to larger animals, it may be wise to complete a few before advancing to bigger game.

Choosing a manikin for your squirrel will be based on its size. Fortunately, squirrel manikins are available in a wide variety of sizes and positions, so finding the pose you want shouldn't be a problem. I'd recommend starting with a squirrel mount in a climbing position, with the squirrel spread out on the surface of a tree trunk, looking over its shoulder. This pose is attractive and keeps things simple—everything is evenly proportioned, the body isn't twisted, the legs aren't in awkward positions, and the mount will be very realistic.

CLIMBING SQUIRREL MOUNT
Materials

- Fleshed and preserved squirrel skin.
- Climbing squirrel manikin of appropriate size.
- Eyes of appropriate size; I prefer hollow bubble eyes because they're easy to position.
- Adhesive on squirrels is optional, and during the learning stages applying adhesive may actually create more problems than it solves. If you do decide to use adhesive, either now or at a later time, do so sparingly.
- Thread and a small needle.
- Small amount of clay.

Mounting Procedures

For mounting a squirrel in the climbing position, I usually prefer a short ventral incision. The reason is simple: The seam is very easy to hide because the stomach and chest of the squirrel will be tight against the tree. Also, due to their small size, they are fairly easy to skin with this method.

But on your first attempt or two it may be easier to use the dorsal incision, which is the one we'll stick with throughout the mounting process discussed in this chapter. Later, once you have a little more experience, you can give the ventral incision a try.

As I touched on in chapter 4, a squirrel's feet may be cut away at the wrist, or skinned to the first joint of each toe. If you choose to separate the feet at the wrist it will be necessary to inject the feet thoroughly with a liquid preservative. And even if you are able to skin to the toes, you'll still need to inject them. Simply insert the needle of a syringe into each toe and inject a small amount of preservative. The toes should swell a little.

It is important to test-fit the skin before you start the mounting process. If the skin doesn't fit, you'll want to know about it before you start making alterations to the manikin. Most suppliers will allow returns as long as a manikin hasn't been altered. If all measurements were taken properly and the manikin is sized as advertised, the skin should fit with no problems.

Once you're certain that the skin will fit, you would normally rough up the surface of the manikin to allow the skin to adhere better. For your first squirrel, though, you can bypass this step because you won't be using adhesive. But when you do use adhesive on a squirrel, or any other mount, it will be necessary to completely rough the surface.

It's also important to adjust the length of the manikin legs at this stage to accommodate the method you've chosen for detaching the feet. Most manikins are sculpted to include the feet, but obviously not the toes. If you've detached the entire foot it will be necessary

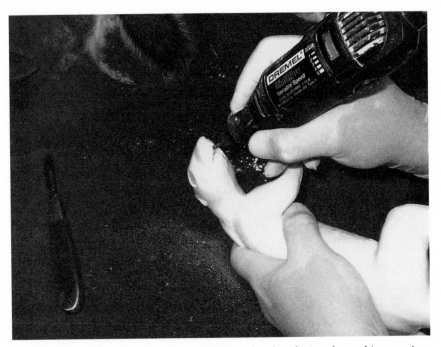

Cut the lip slot wide enough to avoid ripping the skin during the tucking portion.

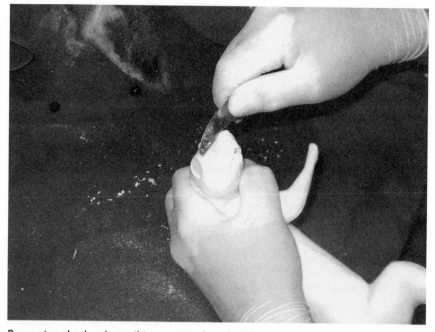

Removing the hard manikin nose and replacing it with clay will help you shape the nose.

Enlarging the eye area of the manikin to accept certain eyes is easily done using a Dremel or similar tool.

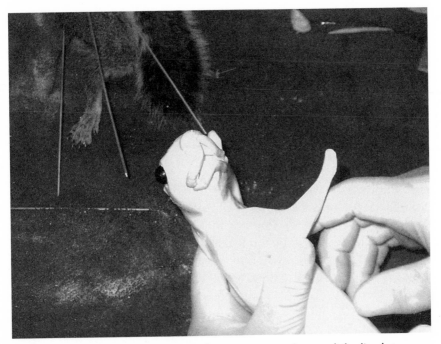

Apply a portion of clay or epoxy to the nose area and around the lip slot.

to cut off the foot portion of the manikin. If you skinned the feet to the toes then you'll probably be able to leave the manikin unaltered.

Next, you'll need to prep the facial area. Because a perfectly sized lip slot and nasal opening would be very small, it is best to oversize both and fill them with small portions of clay to help position the facial skin without tearing it (which might occur should you try to insert the lips into a narrow slot). Use a ⅛-inch drill bit to cut from one corner of the mouth to the other to widen the lip slot, and be sure to follow the pre-sculpted lip line. I usually make this cut at a 45-degree angle rather than at a right angle.

Cut the nose area completely off the manikin. Make a shallow cut straight into the face, just below the nose, then move straight down from the top of the nose toward the lower jaw.

Depending on the eyes you've chosen, you may have to "Dremel" or drill out the eye area to make room. A bubble eye must be inserted significantly deeper into the manikin than a convex/concave eye.

With the mouth slot, nose, and eyeholes adjusted, it's time to fill in these areas with clay. Start by placing a small ball of clay into the area left by the nose. If you happen to apply too much clay you should be able to work it down along each side of the snout. If this isn't possible, use the sculpting tool to pull out a very small portion. Depending on the tightness of the skin, I sometimes attach the clay after pulling the skin onto the manikin. Just open the mouth and place the clay in the appropriate place.

I usually wait until after the skin is pulled onto the manikin before applying clay to the mouth area. If you do it before the skin goes on, a tight skin might distort the clay you've already sculpted.

When you're ready to apply the clay in the mouth area take a small portion, about the size of a marble, and gently roll it between your hands. This roll should be about half the diameter of a pencil. Now place it along the lip line—above and below—completely surrounding the lip slot. During the mounting process this clay will be used to form and contour the lip line. I usually prefer to replace the clay around the mouth with a two-part epoxy, but you shouldn't attempt this until you've gained some experience. Just file it away for future reference. The two-part epoxy, when cured, will be much harder and will hold the lip skin much better than clay.

Also, put a very small amount of clay in the eyeholes. The eyes can't be placed at the correct depth if there is too much clay. If you overfill the holes, lightly push on the eye and scrape off any excess. If you've put way too much clay in the eyehole you may have to gently remove the eye and pull out enough clay to try again. Be careful, though, as hollow bubbles are very fragile. To remove a hollow-bubble eye that has been seated too deeply, use a small needle. Gently insert the needle behind the eye and slowly work it free.

Once the eyes have been inserted at matching depths, you must form an upper and lower brow. This will simulate the musculature that existed on the original skull. I usually shape these brows before sliding the skin onto the manikin. While this may distort the clay you've just sculpted, the damage should be minimal. Also, the eye area is difficult to reach after the skin is in place.

After the face has been prepped and the lengths of each leg adjusted, it is time to insert the manikin into the skin. First, place a small amount of clay on the end of each manikin leg. This aids in forming a smooth leg-to-foot junction. Don't overdo the clay, though, as the legs may appear swelled and unnatural. Your goal should be to create a natural, flowing appearance.

Now pull the skin onto the manikin. For a climbing mount, begin by pulling the skin onto the rear legs. Then continue with the front

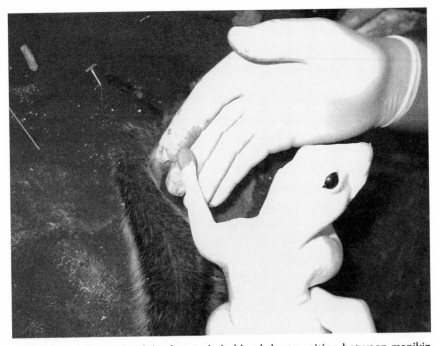

Apply clay to the ends of the feet to help blend the transition between manikin and toes or feet.

legs. Finish by pulling the head of the skin onto the head of the manikin.

The skin should stretch a bit during this process. If it doesn't you may have trouble getting the front half of the skin on the manikin after the rear is on. If this problem occurs, try lengthening the incision along the back. Make certain the incision extends from the base of the tail to the area between the shoulders or slightly forward of the shoulders. This is usually enough to alleviate the problem.

If the incision is already of appropriate length and the skin remains tight, there's something more drastic that you can try. Cut the manikin in half at the midsection, insert each half into the skin, and then reattach the halves. This technique is usually reserved for experienced taxidermists, but if no other options are available it may be worth attempting. When you use more awkward poses, or different incisions on future projects, you may need to remove and reattach manikin limbs to slide the skin on, but for now reattaching the two halves will prove difficult enough.

To split the manikin, make a shallow "V" in the midsection. This will help you realign the halves. Once the manikin halves have been inserted into the skin, join them as neatly as possible. Then use a small amount of Bondo (approximately the size of a marble) to hold the halves in place. Spread it onto the opposing surfaces and press the two halves together, then hold everything in place until the Bondo begins to set up. Set the manikin aside and allow the Bondo to thoroughly harden; ten or fifteen minutes should be sufficient.

With the skin securely in place on the manikin, the next step is to add a support wire to the tail. A small wire like a 14-gauge should be ideal, but a 12 or 16 will work. If the tailbone was slipped free of the skin during the skinning process, simply insert the wire into the tail. (If the tail skin had to be cut during skinning, it can be sewn back on or simply glued with super glue.)

For your first attempt, it may help to push the wire through the end of the tail. This will allow you to quickly adjust the tail length. If the tail is stretched tight it will appear long and thin; shortening it will make it look much more full. Now insert the end of the wire

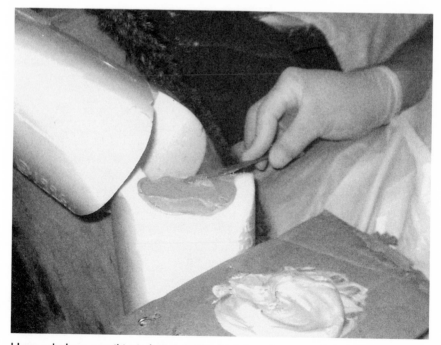

Here a bobcat manikin is being reattached, but the procedure is the same for any type of manikin.

into the manikin to secure it. Push the wire through the back of the manikin at a slight angle. Keep pushing until the wire exits the manikin and then form a "U" in the tip of the wire and tap it back into the manikin. This forms a nice anchor point to prevent slippage.

Now you can sew up the incision. Use short stitches to prevent the skin from "gapping" during the drying process. Also, make certain each stitch is tight and the seam tied off tightly, which will help conceal the seam. Use as small a needle as possible, and dark thread. Be sure to insert the needle into the skin as close to the edge as possible.

Next, position the tail and model the face. Use live reference or photographs to help you achieve lifelike positions.

Before the face is modeled, you'll need to trim the lips and eyes. Then tuck the lips, being sure to correctly position any hair patterns on the rear corners of the mouth, center of the nose, and center of the chin. Begin to work the clay toward the lip slot. After the lips are positioned and the clay smoothed, model the nose.

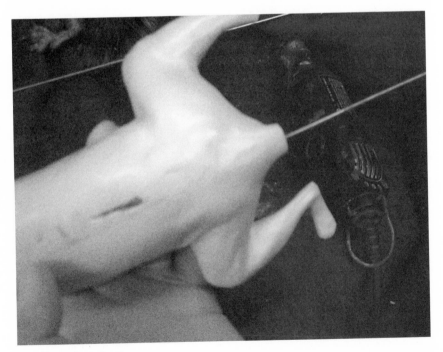

Attaching the tail wire.

Try not to make the nostrils too large, as they will widen during the drying process. A squirrel has a wide space of bare skin directly under the center of its nose due to its large upper front teeth. This bare skin must be tucked into the lip slot before modeling.

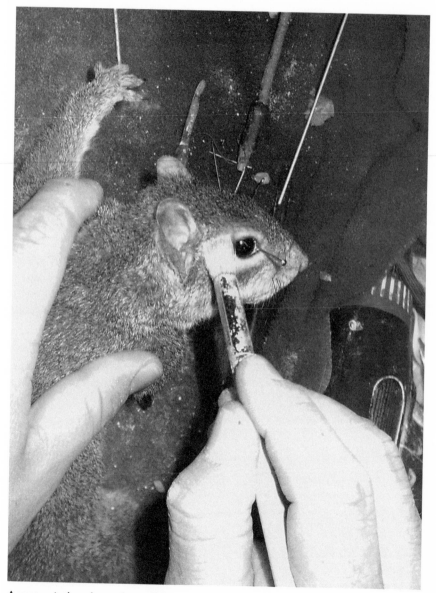

A wet paintbrush works well for cleaning the facial area.

Finish modeling the face by tucking the eyes. Again, make good use of your reference. Most squirrels have a bug-eyed look, so try to duplicate this. Animal eyes are often not completely round, and even if they appear so at a glance, diligent study will reveal slight variations.

This squirrel has been attached to an old post rather than a fancy base.

Now position the ears. Normally, animal ears must be injected or turned so an ear liner can be installed, but because squirrels have small, thin ears, skip the injection and just use a small piece of thin cardboard to sandwich the ear. Position a small paperclip over this cardboard sandwich to hold it in place temporarily. Another effective method is to position the ear with a small amount of clay on the inside. After the clay and ear are dry, the flick of a finger will break the clay free. This won't damage the ear, as it will already be dry and rigid.

Use a wet paintbrush to soften the edges along the lip line, nose, and around the eyes when you have the face modeling complete. The small, wet brush will also remove any clay or other debris from the eyes.

Now you're ready to attach the squirrel to a piece of driftwood. First, line up and drill four small holes into the wood slightly larger than the wire extending from the feet. Pull the wire for each foot through the appropriate hole and bend it over temporarily to secure it.

Finish the mount by making any last-minute adjustments. Make certain that the legs and feet form a smooth junction, that all skin is tucked and appropriately placed and all seams hidden, that the feet appear to naturally grip the wood, and that the overall appearance of the mount is lifelike.

Congratulations! You've hopefully just completed the first of many mounts. Each time you complete a mount the process gets easier and you learn something new. Do the best you can and before long you will be producing high-quality work.

CHAPTER 8

Mounting a Bobcat

The bobcat is a favorite for hunters and non-hunters alike. There's something about this elusive cat that intrigues even those who don't venture afield very often. It may be their exotic appearance. Tan to gold in color, with light to heavy spotting, a bobcat is a trophy anyone would be proud to display in their home. The most impressive cats weigh twenty pounds or more, and some from the Upper Midwest and Canada will tip the scales at more than thirty pounds. Cats this large are highly coveted.

During my first years as a commercial taxidermist it always amazed me how many bobcats came through the doors. Most hunters—if the aren't avid predator hunters—never see a bobcat in the woods. But this is probably why most hunters lucky enough to take a bobcat spend the time and money to preserve it in some way.

I always love to work on bobcats. Besides their beauty, a wide variety of manikin poses are available so you can really get creative.

In this chapter, we're going to look at an open-mouth bobcat mount. As far as basic procedures go, mounting a bobcat isn't that much different from a squirrel. It's just bigger and more time-consuming, with more expensive supplies. The open mouth, however, will give us a chance to add another new element.

A bobcat skin is very durable. I have mounted many bobcats that have been improperly cared for without any major problems. I believe that because a bobcat is a fairly clean animal it doesn't have as much bacteria in the facial area as a fox or coyote.

To keep things simple, we'll stick with a dry-preserved, dorsal-incision bobcat. Adhesive will be applied to the head and legs only. Although some knowledgeable taxidermists will cringe at the procedures I'm detailing here, these methods have been tested again and again by me and many other reputable taxidermists.

If I were mounting this bobcat for a competition, I'd probably opt for a tanned skin (although I did earn a white ribbon at a regional competition in the professional category with a dry-preserved bobcat) and I'd cover the entire manikin with adhesive. But for ordinary display I am perfectly comfortable using the methods described here.

So let's assume the skin has already been fully fleshed, preserved, and test-fitted. Also, if you're using a jawset it should be installed at this point. (See detailed instructions in chapter 10.)

For bobcats, I recommend leaving two joints in the toe during the skinning process. Some taxidermists like to remove all bone, leaving only a claw. But any bone you remove has to be replaced with something, in this case clay, and I feel it is much easier and more accurate to simply leave in place the bone that is already the correct size and shape. Also, because only a very small amount of tissue exists on the toe bones, a liquid preservative will usually be enough to prevent major shrinkage. You may need to make alterations, though, depending on how the manikin's feet are sculpted. Some manikins are designed with the entire foot, including the toes, while others are made only for the ball or primary portion of the foot, no toes included. If the manikin you buy has toes attached, simply cut them off and proceed. Even when I do remove all of the toe bones, I'll still cut the toes from the manikin and replace them with clay so they can be adjusted and custom-fitted.

Before pulling the skin onto the manikin be sure to add a small amount of clay to the feet. This will help the pad to appear full, and it will aid in forming a junction between the toes and feet. Use a portion of clay slightly smaller than a golf ball for each foot, and roll each ball between your hands. Now saturate the clay with dry preservative and drop a roll into each leg. Coating the clay with dry preservative should prevent it from getting stuck halfway down the leg. It should also decrease the drying time of the clay.

After clay has been placed into all four feet, apply a little adhesive to the opening formed on the inside of the skin where the leg exits the body. A small amount should be all that is necessary. This adhesive lubricates the manikin so the skin can be pulled on more easily. Most bobcats can be skinned without cutting the back of the legs. But if it was necessary to split the legs during the skinning process, skip the adhesive; it may only cause problems.

Now pull the skin onto the legs. When each leg is almost fully inserted try to pull the skin onto the head. Fortunately, after skinning,

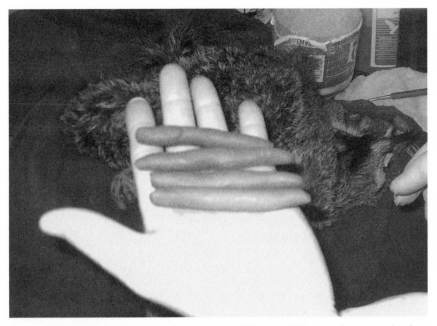

Four small lengths of clay, one for each foot. These will be used to join the feet of the bobcat to the manikin.

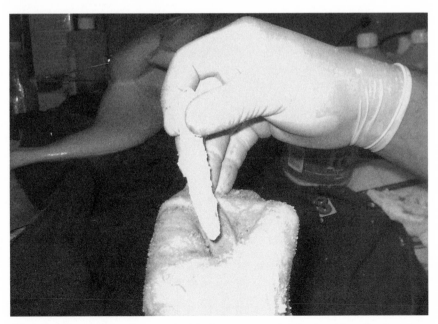

After the piece of clay is coated with dry preservative, it should easily drop into place, alleviating any sticking that may otherwise occur.

most bobcat mouths are large enough to allow the manikin head to be pulled through after the skin has been placed on the manikin. This means that you can wait to install the eyes and any clay around the face until just prior to finishing the mount. If for some reason the skin can't be pulled onto the head after the legs are inserted, you may have to make the dorsal incision longer. If the incision already reaches from the shoulder (or slightly forward of this point) rearward to the base of the tail, the head of the manikin may need to be removed.

Removing and reattaching the head is a fairly simple procedure. With a shallow "V" cut, detach the head and neck at a point slightly forward of the shoulders. Now slide the head and neck of the manikin into the head and neck of the skin.

Thoroughly mix a portion of Bondo approximately the size of a golf ball. Realign the head and place the Bondo in the joint area between the neck and shoulders. Press the two pieces together, making certain that nothing has shifted up or down. Hold the joint together until the Bondo begins to harden, then remove any excess

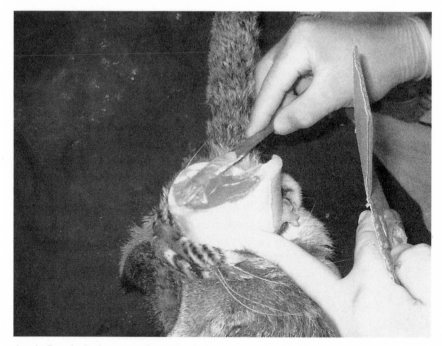

Apply Bondo before attaching the head.

that may have squeezed out around the seam. Allow ten to fifteen minutes for the Bondo to cure.

The last task to complete before sewing is to pull the tail onto the tail wire. Most bobcat manikins come with a preexisting tail wire. If yours doesn't, simply angle a size 12 wire upward through the back, then form a "U" in the end, and anchor fully by tapping the wire back into the manikin.

A bobcat's tail is easily slipped during skinning, so no sewing should be necessary. Simply slide the wire into the tail opening. I used to try to get an exact tail length estimate, then clip the tail wire, but I've found it easier to push the wire through the tip of the tail, adjust the length during the mounting process, and then clip the wire after any final adjustments or drying.

With the skin pulled onto the legs, tail, and head, you should be ready to pull the skin around the body and start sewing. If your early measurements were accurate, the skin should come together easily. For larger animals, it is sometimes wise to start at the tail and work your way forward while also closing the seam at the opposite end

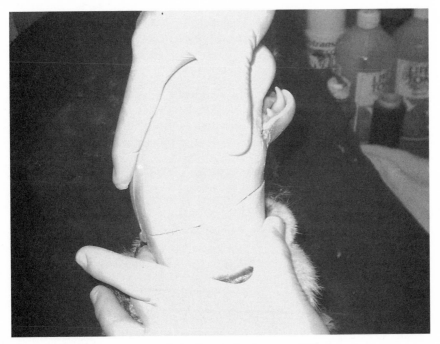

Hold the head in position until the Bondo begins to solidify.

of the incision. The two seams should meet in the middle, and this procedure will help prevent any puckers due to uneven sewing. If you remembered to make small indicator holes or cuts to aid in lining up the sides of the seam the sewing process should be quick and easy.

Now it's time to model the face. Pull the skin of the head slightly forward of the manikin head, far enough so that the ear bases can be reached. As mentioned earlier, most animal ears should be turned to the edge. But for the small, thin ears of a bobcat, remember master taxidermist Tab Hinton's trick. Instead of turning the ear all the way to the end, separate it only enough to insert a small amount of clay at the base. Then form the shape of the ear base. The remainder of the ear can just be injected with liquid preservative.

The simplest and cheapest liquid preservative formula is half denatured alcohol and half water. Insert the needle of a small syringe into the center of the back of the ear. Don't allow the tip of the needle to exit the other side. Now inject the solution slowly until it feels like the entire ear has received fluid. It may take a couple of full syringes to completely saturate the ear. Remove the syringe from the needle—leaving the needle in place—and refill, then reattach it and inject the additional preservative. By leaving the tip of the needle in place while you reload syringes, you only have to make one hole. And be sure to wear latex gloves and protective eyewear when you're working with liquid preservative.

Slide the skin back onto the manikin head. Then open the mouth and slowly push the skin toward the back of the head. If the skin is very tight, go slowly, but if the skin won't go on don't force it or it may tear. Even if the skin can't be pulled to the back of the head it can usually be pulled high enough to model the eyes.

If at all possible, push the skin into position all the way to the back of the head. This allows you to cut small holes in the manikin on the sides of the head for the ear butts. Use a dull knife to carve out the holes, which should be about two inches in diameter and about an inch deep.

A great method for determining the location of these holes is to study a bobcat skull before it has been cleaned. Notice where the ear canals are located, and then try to position your holes in the same areas. This should put the ears very close to where they need to be. Next, place clay into these holes. Use enough to fill each hole slightly below level with the remainder of the head. This leaves room for the ear butts.

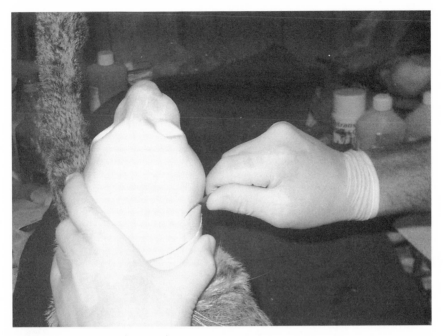

Cutting ear holes in the manikin.

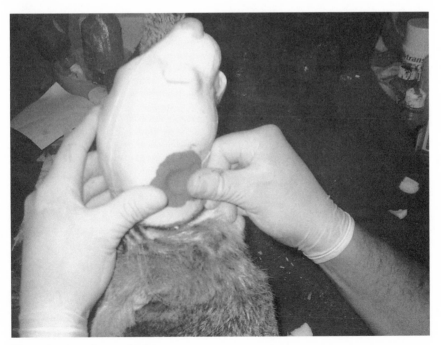

Place clay into the ear holes.

Now install the eyes. The presculpted eye positions on most good manikins are very accurate, but if they aren't you may have to make some alterations. For this reason, I'd recommend that a beginner purchase a high-quality manikin from a reputable source—there's already enough to worry about without having to tweak the eyes.

Start by placing a small portion of clay into the hollowed-out side of the glass eye, then press it tightly into position. The clay will help the eye stick to the manikin. I can't stress enough the importance of checking references to make sure the eyes look natural, but as a general rule the slit in a bobcat's eye will slant slightly toward the center of its head. This slant is barely noticeable, but it is there.

When each eye is in place, roll out a small portion of clay about half the size of a pencil and flatten it around each eye. The corner of a bobcat's eye that is closest to the nose is slightly lower than the other corner. To duplicate this, beginning with the mount's right eye, place one end of the clay roll at about four o'clock, then slowly work it into position as you take the other end to ten o'clock. Finish by applying a smaller roll to the bottom of the eye. But this time start at the corner closest to the nose and apply the remainder to the bottom of the eye, again stopping at ten o'clock.

Repeat this operation for the left eye. But make the low corner eight o'clock and the high corner two o'clock.

Next, cut the rigid nose off the manikin with a "V" cut in front and across the top. Or Dremel away the material in the nose area. Replace the foam with a small ball of clay and sculpt a natural-looking nose.

It may also be beneficial to remove the foam material on each side of the upper jaw and replace it with clay. This is where the whisker roots are located, and the clay will allow you to make adjustments without the skin drying and forcing the whiskers to lie flat.

After you've placed all the clay and finished the preliminary sculpting, apply a small amount of two-part epoxy adhesive to the head. It is best to avoid getting this adhesive on your hands or the animal's fur. But if you do, it can usually be removed with soap and water or lacquer thinner if you get to it quickly. Apply the adhesive sparingly with a butter knife. If there is too much, it will ooze out and cause problems. Now pull the skin into its proper position on the head.

It's time to begin the initial positioning of all facial features. Trim any excess eye, nostril, and lip skin. Trim ⅛ inch past the eyelid. For the nostrils and lip skin, simply trim off any ragged edges. You may need the excess for tucking.

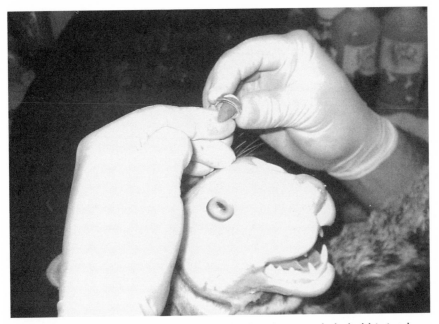

Place a small amount of clay into the back of each eye to help hold it in place.

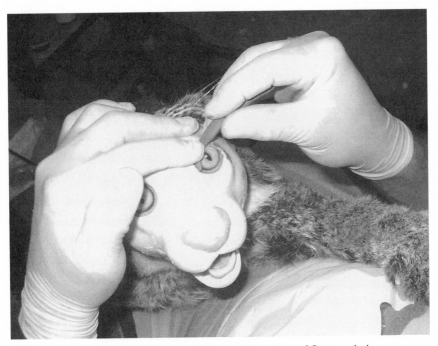

Begin to model around each eye using a small portion of flattened clay.

To mount an open-mouth animal, I begin the positioning in the mouth area, being careful to account for any hair patterns. Primary hair patterns include the center of the chin, the center of the nose, and the rear corners of the mouth.

Look closely at references and you'll notice that along the upper jaw, skin with hair goes to the edge, but on the lower jaw a lot of hairless lip is evident. Try to duplicate this. Position the lip line and lock it into place by tucking any excess skin between the lip and the jawset. Anchor firmly using small brads or nails. Use needlenose pliers to insert the small nails into the manikin, and angle the nails toward the inside of the mouth. Insert a nail every half inch, making sure that the skin will be secure during the drying process.

Next, you'll need to form the nose and adjust the nostrils using a sculpting tool. If there is too much clay just remove a small amount; if too little, add some. This is most easily done through a nostril hole. Your goal should be to form a fleshy, slightly rounded nose that isn't flat or bumpy.

On to the eyes, which can really bring animals to life. Carefully tuck the excess from the eyelids under the clay that surrounds each

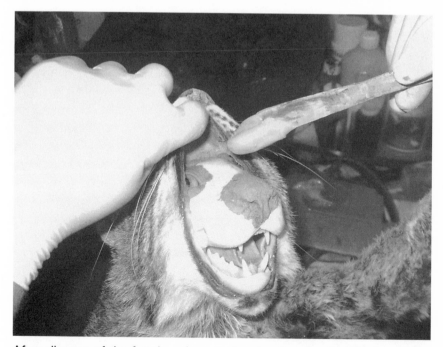

After all areas of the face have been sculpted and replaced with clay, apply a small amount of adhesive.

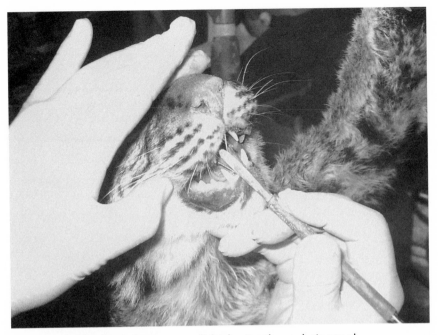

Placement of lip skin is best accomplished using the sculpting tool.

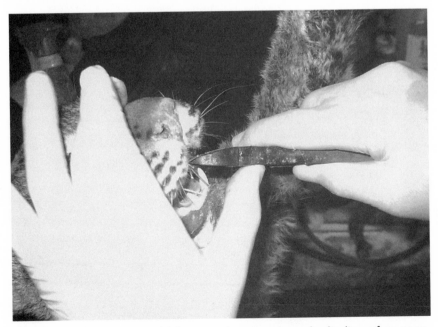

Needle-nose pliers are useful for inserting pins along the lip line of an open-mouthed mount.

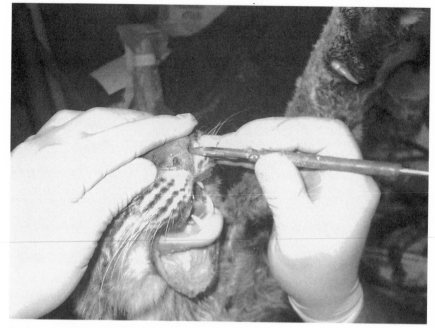

Preliminary shaping of the nose.

Tuck and adjust the eye area.

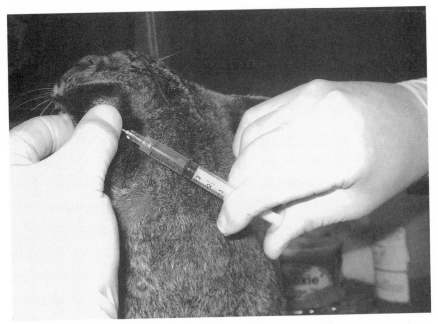

With the preliminary modeling complete, it's time to inject the ear.

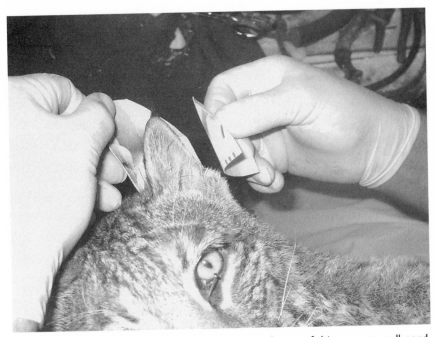

Finish the ears by sandwiching them between two layers of thin precut cardboard.

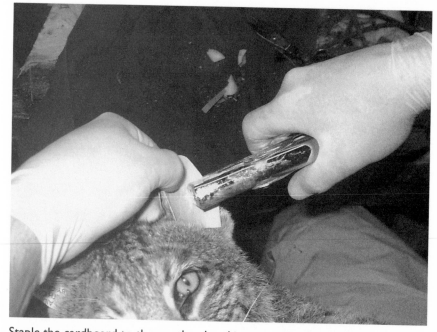

Staple the cardboard to the ear, then bend it to an appropriate shape.

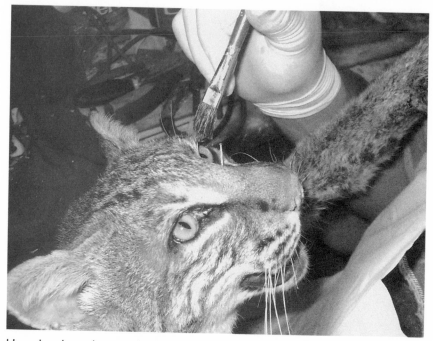

Use a brush to clean up the facial area.

eye. Again, spend some time studying references and try to dupli-cate the eye of a live animal. Remember that the corner near the nose is generally lower than the corner near the side of the head.

After the eyes are tucked, position the ears by sticking a thumb into the ear butt and pressing it in place. This should fully seat the ear base. If you took the time to make sure the holes were cut accu-rately in the sides of the head, the ears should look good. Sandwich each ear between a thin piece of cardboard (cereal boxes or chew-ing tobacco boxes are ideal for this), staple in place, and adjust to a proper shape.

All that's left to do is clean and soften the eyes and the sur-rounding skin with a wet paintbrush, making sure to work around the nose and along the lip line, as well.

Take one last look to make final adjustments to the ears and to position and shape the feet and legs. No bulges or odd contours should be noticeable. Once everything is complete, put the bobcat aside to dry properly.

CHAPTER 9

Mounting a Coyote

Despite long-term efforts at predator control, coyote populations have increased and expanded in recent decades. Nearly every state now has a huntable population of these salt-and-pepper-colored song dogs. Coyotes make nice mounts, particularly those with beautifully thick winter coats. And taxidermy suppliers stock manikins in a variety of poses.

We'll mount our coyote on all fours, looking to the right—nothing extraordinary, but a nice-looking angle. You could also try something a little more dramatic, such as howling, jumping for prey, sitting like a dog, or even running after prey. It's even possible to alter a manikin for unconventional poses, although severe alterations usually require a bit of experience. Get several mounts under your belt before tinkering too much; everyone has to start somewhere.

Although I earlier touched on the idea of removing and reattaching manikin parts only when necessary on smaller game, you'll find that most larger manikins will be cut in half before being shipped, to save space. It's very simple to reattach the parts, though. Just mix up an appropriate amount of Bondo, apply some to both halves in the area to be joined, align the halves, and hold them together. To strengthen this bond you may want to insert long screws into the joint at an angle. These will hold the two halves together while the Bondo dries and will add some strength to the joint.

The techniques for mounting a coyote are basically the same ones we used on the squirrel and bobcat—and these procedures will work just as well for all game, large and small. For the coyote, the primary differences are that the tail and legs must be sewn and ear liners placed into the ears. All other procedures are nearly identical. So instead of rehashing these, let's move on to the new elements.

After the standard fleshing and preservation procedures have been completed, install ear liners into the ears. Although plenty of commercial ear liners are available, I recommend using Bondo, which allows you to leave in the ear cartilage. Also, if an ear is oddly shaped, the Bondo will conform to it, creating a perfect ear liner. It is also convenient, as most taxidermists have a can of Bondo somewhere in the shop. The downside is that some taxidermists get the ears too thick. And Bondo can make things messy in a hurry if you aren't careful.

To keep things simple, just work on one ear at a time. Make certain the ear is turned fully, all the way to the edge. Now pull the ear base through the mouth of the coyote skin. To prevent contamination spray a small amount of window cleaner on the surrounding hair. This will stop the Bondo from adhering to the hair.

Mix a small amount of Bondo, about half the size of a golf ball, and insert the mixture well into the ear. (To prevent making thick ears, use a little less Bondo than you think you'll need.) Now begin to form a natural ear shape. Pull the tip of the ear so the entire ear is in a normal position, then slowly work the Bondo into all parts of the ear. If any air is left in the tip, puncture a small hole in it with a needle.

The goal is to form a thin, smooth, natural ear before any hardening takes place. Once the Bondo begins to set up, shaping will become difficult. If hardening begins before you've gotten the shape you want, invert the ear, discard the Bondo, and try again. Don't let the Bondo harden until you have the ear you want.

Coyote ears are sensitive, and the curing Bondo can create a lot of heat, which can cause slippage. And continuous handling doesn't help. So move as quickly as possible during this procedure. Having your coyote commercially tanned will alleviate most slippage problems.

Once both ears are formed and hardened, place a small portion of clay around the base of each ear. This will be used to form a smooth junction between the ear and the manikin.

Now pull the skin onto the manikin. If the head of the skin won't easily slide onto the manikin head, make the incision along the back longer, or separate the head of the manikin from its body. Then, after inserting the manikin head into the head area of the skin, rejoin the manikin.

Pull the sides of the back incision together, using pins to hold the skin in position. These can be removed as the sewing progresses. When you're finished sewing up the back incision, close the tail incision and the legs.

I usually start with the legs because they are the most difficult. The leg skin of a coyote is thin so go slowly and use short, tight stitches. Start at the back edge of the footpad and sew upward, toward the body. If you kept these cuts as short as possible during the skinning process you'll be able to minimize excessive and unnecessary sewing.

Finish up the sewing by working on the tail. Most manikins have wire tails already attached, but if not, it's easy to do yourself. (See chapter 8 for details.) For competition-quality mounts, I'd recommend wrapping the wire to rebuild the shape of the larger bones and tissue, but for commercial work you can simply wrap the skin of the tail around the tail wire and close the incision. Sewing is the best method for this, as it produces a clean, smooth seam. But you can also use super glue. As most incisions are made on the underside of the tail, super glue shouldn't be noticeable at all, and it will save some time. Just place a small bead along one edge of the skin and press the sides together, working in short sections to avoid problems.

You can now concentrate on the facial area, using the same methods discussed for squirrels and bobcats. Apply adhesive

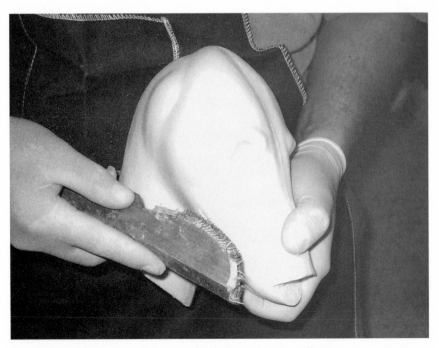

Rough the slick surface of the manikin before applying adhesive.

Pull the skin onto the head so the face can be sculpted.

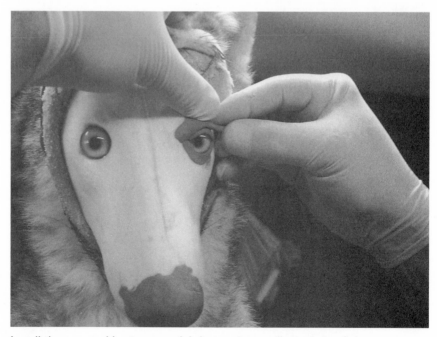

Install the eyes and begin to model them using small portions of clay.

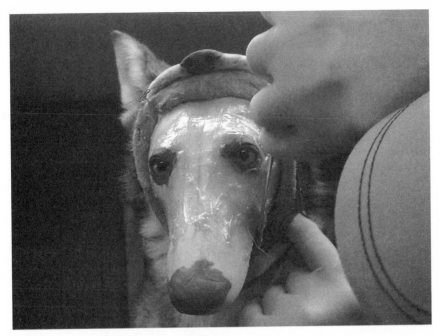

Apply a thin layer of adhesive to the head.

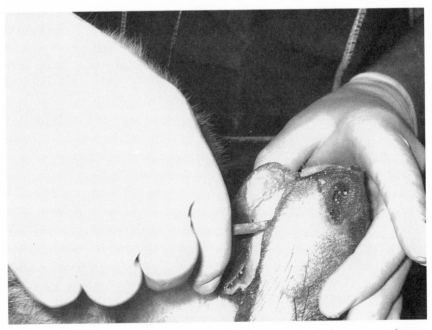

Begin tucking the lips. It is best to start with the upper lip before proceeding to the lower lip.

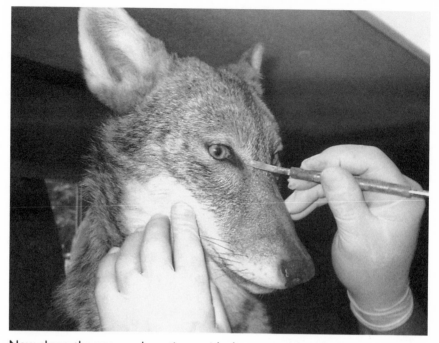

Now shape the nose and continue with the eyes, again referring to reference photos.

sparingly to the head. For dry-preserved skins, I recommend a two-part epoxy adhesive; for tanned skins either a two-part epoxy adhesive or an adhesive formulated for tanned skin.

Trim the eyelids, nostrils, and lips; then tuck. Use a wet paint-brush to clean and soften the eyes, nose, and lip line. Position the ears, smooth the transitions between feet and legs, position the tail, and look the mount over thoroughly before setting it aside for proper drying. The only variations to these procedures will come from dealing with the particular appearances of individual species. As always, this can best be understood by studying reference photos. A coyote's eyes obviously aren't shaped like those of a bobcat or a deer. Use references to achieve a natural look.

Another difference from animal to animal is mood—or, in taxidermy, the intended mood. For example, if a coyote is supposed to look ferocious, this can't be accomplished with a naturally closed mouth and normally shaped eyes. The mouth would need to curl into a snarl, whether open or closed. The eyes would need to carry a heavier than usual brow to convey an aggressive posture. The ears would need to be laid back a little or a lot, depending on how aggressive you want the coyote to be. And even the tail would need to be tucked tightly between the legs.

The nuances of each pose are endless, which is part of what makes taxidermy so enjoyable. Pick the pose you want and study every detail of the animal to create the desired appearance.

CHAPTER

10

Mount Finishing

When the mounting procedure is complete, you'll need to put the mount aside for a short time to allow it to dry thoroughly. After this drying stage, additional shrinkage will be minimal, and the paints and epoxies you'll need to apply next will adhere much better. Drying times will vary from project to project. The type of animal being mounted, humidity and temperature, and the preservation method will all be factors.

Some taxidermists use a drying room, which is an airtight room with a dehumidifier and a large fan. Such a room should leave you with a completely dry mount in two to four days. Drying times without these special considerations will be much longer.

For the beginner who doesn't have a drying room, it will be best to let the mount sit in a room that is sixty to eighty degrees with humidity as low as possible. Where I live, in the South, the humidity is rarely below eighty percent during spring and summer, but at a temperature of seventy degrees most mounts will dry without problems. But drying a mount in a humid and extremely hot or cold environments can cause major problems.

To see if your mount is dry, insert a finger into the ear. The ear butt or clay positioned in this area is usually the last thing to dry, so if it feels okay chances are the mount is completely dry. Allow at least three weeks before doing any finish work with your first few mounts, just to be on the safe side. Later on, experience will help you determine when a mount is dry.

When dry, you will notice that the skin of the mount has lost much of its natural color around the eyes, on the nose, and within the ears. This has to be replaced. Also, shrinkage occurs as a mount dries, and we'll have to rebuild these shrunken areas. Proper fleshing will have minimized this shrinkage, so if the mount shrinks considerably at this stage you will know that you need to be more attentive to fleshing on the next mount.

If shrinkage is minimal, you've done a great job. The only additional area that would need to be finished on some mounts is an open mouth. The lip line will have to be blended into the jawset, and the teeth on some animals will have to be stained for a lifelike appearance.

The supplies you'll need to complete the finish work include paints, an airbrush, epoxies, and paintbrushes for blending the epoxies. The paints are obviously used to replace or touch up any areas with color loss, while the epoxies will be used to rebuild shrunken areas. Several brands of paint and epoxy are available at most taxidermy suppliers.

Some veteran taxidermists insist on oil paints that have to be brushed on, and wax instead of epoxy for rebuilding shrunken areas. Many of these taxidermists produce quality work with these methods. But many other professionals, including me, prefer an airbrush loaded with a paint formulated specifically for taxidermy. Also, two-part epoxies seem to adhere better to the mount than wax and hold paint much better than other alternatives.

Most suppliers offer mammal paint kits. These kits usually contain every color you'll need for general finishing. During the learning stages these paints should be just fine, but as you gain experience you'll discover additional colors that aid in bringing a mount to life. You can purchase water-based and lacquer-based taxidermy paints. But I don't recommend mixing the two. For example, don't apply a coat of water-based paint then spray a lacquer over the top of it. You'll avoid most finishing problems by sticking to just one or the other. So which one is right for you? Well, only you can decide; but I prefer lacquers.

One major advantage of lacquer paints is that they dry much faster than water-based paints, often as soon as they are applied. The downside to using lacquers is the health risk they pose and their flammability. You should wear a respirator mask whenever you apply taxidermy paint, but this is particularly important with lacquers. Also, make sure that there is adequate ventilation in your workroom, to help dissipate the flammable lacquer fumes.

Many taxidermists like water-based paints because they are not as harmful to the user's health and aren't flammable. I'd still recommend that you use a respirator with water-based paint, but it isn't mandatory. You can also thin a water-based paint with plain water, which is very convenient, or acetone. The major disadvantage is the slow dry time. It may take a minute or two for a water-based paint to dry, and this will depend greatly on what is used to thin the paint and how much is used.

The type of epoxy you choose doesn't matter too much, as most brands are very similar. They consist of two substances that are slightly stiffer than clay. To activate the epoxy, mix the two parts together in a 50/50 ratio. For best results, mix thoroughly. Most epoxies will provide an hour or more of working time. Another popular material for rebuilding shrunken areas is epoxy clay, which has a nice texture and adheres well to paint.

MOUNT FINISHING 101

The finishing process for any type of mount follows the same general pattern, although the color scheme may change slightly from one animal to another. Also, the interior of the mouth on an open-mouth mount will obviously have to be finished.

To prep the mount for finishing, brush the eyes, nose, and inner ear areas with a small wire brush. This should clear away any stray particles or underlying epidermis that may still be loosely attached to the skin's surface. Be careful around the glass eyes, though, as they can be scratched easily.

Next, thoroughly brush the entire mount, and then use compressed air to rid the mount of loose hair. These cleaning steps are very important because if you paint over anything loose that might later fall off a bare spot will show.

After a mount has been thoroughly cleaned, rebuild any shrunken areas with epoxy. Start by looking closely at each eyelid. During the mounting process the eyelid will lie against the eye. But as the mount dries it will start to pull away. How much it pulls away depends on the thoroughness of the fleshing job. If the area was fleshed properly this gap between eye and eyelid will probably be less than $\frac{1}{16}$ inch. But on a poorly fleshed mount this gap may widen to more than $\frac{1}{8}$ inch.

Fill in this area with well-mixed epoxy. First, place small amounts of epoxy between the eye and eyelid with a sculpting tool, using the flat end of the tool to force the filler into the crevice. Continue

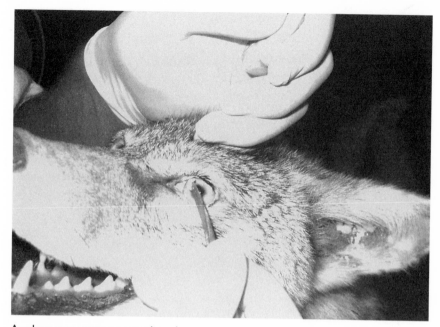

Apply epoxy putty to any shrunken areas.

around the entire eye. If the corner of the eye or the tear duct was cut or torn during the fleshing process, now is the time to rebuild this area.

Once all areas around the eye are filled in or repaired, remove the excess with the sculpting tool and use a thick paintbrush dipped in lacquer thinner to smooth and blend the epoxies to the skin of the eyelid. If this is done properly it should be difficult to see where the epoxy and skin junction is without the help of the color difference.

The nose is another key area. If the nose pad was fleshed thoroughly it should be smooth, very similar to a live animal. If there are slight imperfections use the filler to smooth the surface. But if the nose is very wrinkled or bumpy I'd recommend leaving it alone and continuing. A poorly mounted nose looks better than a bulbous, rounded mess, which is probably what would result from trying to fix it with epoxy. Chalk it up to experience and dedicate yourself to fleshing more thoroughly on the next mount.

The interior of each nostril will definitely need some epoxy filler. Insert a small amount of epoxy into each nostril with the sculpting tool, and begin to shape the interiors like the reference photos

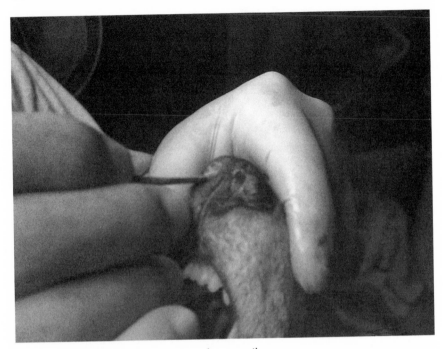

Place a small amount of epoxy into the nostril.

you've studied. Dip the end of the sculpting tool into some thinner during the shaping process; this reduces tackiness and will help you achieve a smooth shape.

The lower lip is the last prominent feature that may require rebuilding. If the bottom lip shows with a closed-mouth mount, this area will usually need to be rebuilt slightly to simulate a fleshy look. Most small game and predators do not naturally show a bottom lip, but some do. Larger animals like deer, elk, and bear nearly always do. Study your references because if it is required a fleshy lower lip can add that extra believability to a mount.

To rebuild the lower lip, roll a very small portion of epoxy between your fingers, forming a rounded length. Apply this to the lower lip area and use the sculpting tool to gradually blend and smooth the epoxy. Don't overdo the lip; you want the added epoxy to flow naturally from the skin. To accomplish this natural look it may be a good idea to form the lip slightly smaller that what seems just right. After you have the general shape of the lip line, continue brushing to finish smoothing and blending.

The rebuilding process should now be complete for a closed-mouth mount.

OPEN-MOUTH MOUNTS

Open-mouth mounts are very popular and can add something special to any game room or trophy collection. Through the years, I have seen plenty of mouth work. Good mouth work adds realism to the mount but, needless to say, poor mouth work does just the opposite because it's so visible. On some of the worst mounts I've seen, the taxidermist didn't even attempt to fill the gap between the skin and jawset. And this gap is obvious to anyone who even glances at such a mount.

Most jawsets will be installed prior to the mounting process, but you may choose to install the jawset after the mount is dry (if this is possible on your mount). Installing the jawset after the mount is dry allows you more room in which to work within the mouth. But if you choose to install the jawset after mounting you still have to make certain that the jawset will fit into the open mouth of the manikin before mounting.

The top of the head is removable on most open-mouth manikins, so test-fitting the jawset should be easy. These manikins are very convenient to work with, as both the top and bottom sections of the mouth are designed to accept most jawsets. But the mouth area on some manikins is filled in with foam that you'll have to cut out or Dremel away, and in some situations they are the only ones available for a particular size.

To install the jawset into a manikin with a removable headpiece, remove the top section of the head. Now make sure that the lower jaw fits properly into the bottom portion of the manikin. Most open-mouth manikins will come with a recommended jawset. If you follow this recommendation the jawset should fit with no alteration. If not, you may need to make some slight modifications.

Assuming you've checked carefully for a good fit, the lower jaw should be easy to attach. Mix a small portion of Bondo and spread it on the bottom side of the lower section of the jawset. Next, apply a small amount to the bottom on the manikin. Attach the two, check your alignment, and hold everything in place until the Bondo begins to solidify.

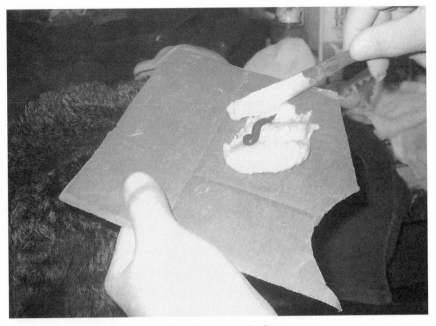

Mix an appropriate amount of Bondo to attach the jawset.

Apply Bondo to the lower section of the jawset.

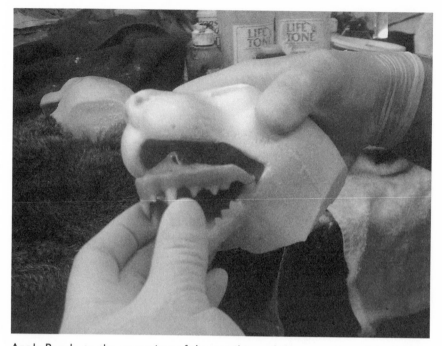

Apply Bondo to the upper jaw of the manikin and the upper jaw of the jawset.

Repeat this procedure for the top jaw.

Now join the top portion of the head with the top of the jaw attached to the body of the manikin (which has the lower jaw already attached). Place a small portion of Bondo between these two sections and press them together. Check the alignment and hold in place until the Bondo begins to harden. This will complete the installation of the jawset.

To strengthen the jawset and its junction with the head, rough up the areas to which Bondo will be applied. Digging out a couple of shallow chunks in the center of the attachment area with a sculpting tool also improves strength. You can even insert a three-inch screw through the upper portion of the head and into the lower portion before the Bondo hardens.

Finish by rolling out a small portion of epoxy between the jaw line and artificial jawset. Smooth the epoxy with a sculpting tool. Wetting the sculpting tool will help prevent sticking. After smoothing the junction, let the area dry and apply paint until the correct color has been achieved. Avoid overpainting.

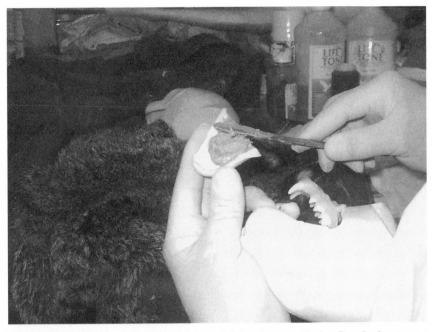

Apply Bondo to the lower jaw then hold in place until the Bondo begins to harden.

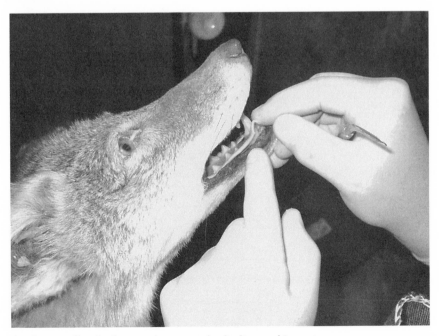

Apply a small roll of epoxy between the lip line and jawset.

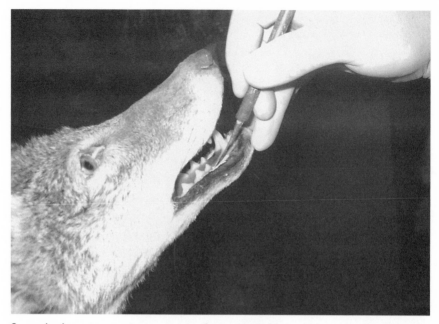

Smooth the epoxy using a wet sculpting tool. Use water instead of lacquer thinner to avoid removing the color from a prepainted jawset.

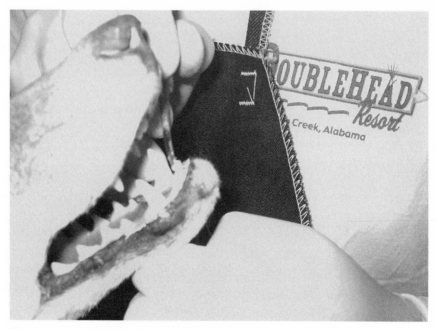

Continue smoothing with a wet brush.

Use a guard when you paint the lip line to minimize errors.

Most open-mouth mounts are completed with plastic, acrylic, or wax jawsets that sit conveniently in the open mouth of the manikin. But there is another alternative.

Mouth Inserts

In addition to conventional jawsets, which require more finishing work, various mouth cups or inserts are now available. Mouth cups are presculpted inserts that have fleshy, accurate lip lines and highly detailed mouth interiors, including the back of the throat. Some inserts come prefinished just like some jawsets do. With a prefinished insert all you'll need to do is blend the junction between the skin and the insert. Instead of applying epoxy to form the gum and interior lip, you'll just use a very small portion of epoxy to join the preserved skin to the lip line.

Installing a mouth cup is very easy. The skin is joined to the insert along the lip line where the haired area meets the hair-free area. This joint is initially made during the mounting process. Instead of attaching the hairless lip skin, as is normally done, it is removed prior to mounting.

Removing this unwanted skin is very easy. Cut the skin with a scalpel one or two millimeters to the hairless side of the line formed by the hair and hairless junction. Make this cut around the entire mouth. Then, during the mounting process, make sure any hair patterns line up before joining the skin to the insert. These hair patterns are generally most evident at the rear corners of the mouth and in the center of the chin and nose. Make certain that the joint area is very tight, without any gaps.

The skin may pull slightly back from the insert during the drying process. You can fill this with epoxy, but your goal should be to keep this separation to a minimum. To aid in locking the skin tightly to the insert use a five-minute epoxy during mounting. This will secure the skin before any drying takes place. Spread a thin layer of this pasty, textured epoxy along the area adjacent to the presculpted lip with a sculpting tool or butter knife. How wide you make this epoxy line will depend on the size of the animal being mounted, but spread the epoxy at least ¼ inch or more if possible. Be careful using five-minute epoxy, though, as it can make a terrible, unfixable mess.

After drying, finishing the junction of the skin and mouth insert should be relatively simple if the mounting process went smoothly. Use the same two-part epoxy you used for the eyes and nose. These two-part epoxies are available in several different colors. For most small game I would recommend using black, as some lips are black all the way to the interior of the mouth—the coyote being one example. If the skin is much lighter it may be better to use pink or an uncolored natural gray.

Mix a small amount of the colored epoxy and roll it out in the shape of a pencil. Pinch off a little and continue to roll it between your hands; this will increase the length and lessen the diameter. When the diameter seems right, begin laying the epoxy into the crevice at the line formed by the skin-to-insert junction. Immediately blend it into the lip line and the skin.

If the insert is prepainted, dip the sculpting tool in water rather than lacquer thinner to avoid removing any paint along the lip of the insert. Be sure to completely fill all gaps along this junction, then use a paintbrush dipped in water (again to avoid removing paint) to continue blending. If further blending is necessary you can use 100-grit sandpaper. Dampen the sandpaper with water and lightly press it into the joint area. This will give texture to the slick, finished surface of the epoxy.

When the epoxy is shaped to your satisfaction, you may notice that some paint is needed to soften the edge where opposing colors meet. Start with a very small amount of paint and continue adding until a smooth color flow is achieved.

Most suppliers that offer mouth inserts also have specific forms they attach to. These make assembly much easier. Otherwise, severe alterations will have to be made, and it's difficult to do a good job with this unless you have a lot of experience. So if you choose to use a mouth insert, make certain you also buy a manikin that is designed to accept it. If not, you should probably stick with a conventional jawset.

ARTIFICIAL NOSES

It's best to mount the nose conventionally when you're just starting out, but once you've mastered this you may want to try an artificial nose. With an artificial nose, the interior of each nostril is already sculpted for you. Also, the outer surface is fleshy and highly detailed, giving it a very realistic look.

Incorporating an artificial nose is very simple. Actually, some mouth inserts come with a nose already attached. If not, just cut out an appropriate spot on the manikin and apply a small amount of five-minute epoxy. Once the artificial nose is attached to the manikin the mounting procedures are identical to those we used for joining skin to a jaw insert. Just be sure to use the appropriate size and line up any hair patterns, and things should go smoothly.

Artificial noses also make excellent 3-D references for sculpting your own noses.

PAINTING

When the mount has been thoroughly cleaned and all shrunken areas dealt with, it's time to apply a base coat of sealer. This will help the paints, which you'll apply next, adhere better. Two or three light layers of sealer are better than one thick layer. Use this sealer in the areas surrounding the eye, the interior of the ears, and the nose pad.

A dark brown color can be used for most of the painting on small game and predators. This includes the areas around the eyes and the nose. Although the nose may appear black in reference photos, dark brown will probably be closer to the original color.

Some other colors that might prove useful include a burnt sienna for the nose of a bobcat, black for the lip line or nose of a coyote or raccoon, and flesh mixed with off-white for the interior of the ears.

When the sealer is dry, start adding color according to references you've studied, or the paint schedule for the animal you're mounting, which can sometimes be obtained through taxidermy suppliers. As you gain experience you'll probably come up with your own paint schedule for each species you work on.

Don't forget that the primary goal of the taxidermist is to make the mount look natural, not painted. So be very sparing when you

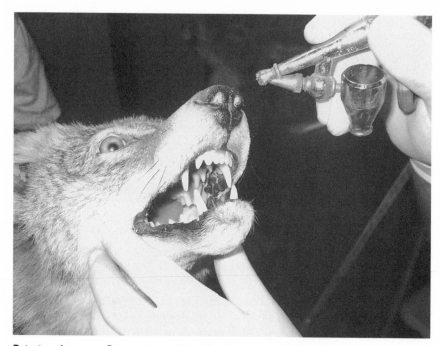

Painting the nose. Repeat procedure for the eyes and mouth.

apply paint. While you're still in the beginner stage, it's probably best to stop short of what appears to be enough paint. You can always add a little more, but you should try to avoid overpainting.

After all paints have dried, apply a sealant. This will add durability to the paint and help avoid paint loss. Apply basecoat sealer around the eyes. Then carefully apply a thin coat of satin to the eyelid, which should appear semi-wet. Next, spray the interior of the ear with satin to duplicate the waxy appearance most animal ears have.

Finally, use a gloss on the nose. This is the only area on which I use a gloss. Some taxidermists like to use gloss around the eyes and the ears too, but I think this adds a cartoonish quality. Sometimes even the nose will naturally appear dry. If you prefer a dry nose, apply a satin or basecoat sealer over the paint and skip the gloss.

All finish work should now be complete.

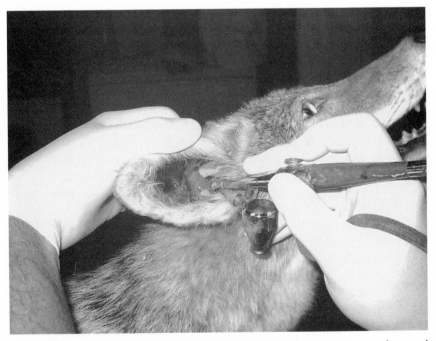

Paint the interior of the ear very lightly, only enough to cover any damaged epidermis that may be present.

11

Base Building

Until now, we've directed all our efforts toward producing a quality mount. And if you've worked carefully, even your first mount will be a work of art. But part of what makes an animal unique is its surroundings or habitat. I have seen many mounts that were simply attached to a board. Not only is this tacky, it detracts from the mount. On the other hand, I have seen average mounts attached to very realistic scenery bases that created a beautiful overall display.

Most top-notch taxidermists put as much effort into their base work as they do their taxidermy skills. Stop in at any state, regional, or national competition and you will quickly see how painstakingly detailed bases can be. Many competitions even have a category just for the bases.

The nicest bases generally include a finished hardwood frame that surrounds the habitat. But such a polished, modern look isn't always necessary. Sometimes a base made out of planks from an old barn can better accentuate a mount, giving it just the right rustic look.

Also, the species of animal and its size and pose will dictate the style of display. A climbing squirrel would look unnatural if it was attached to a two-foot square base. A squirrel should either be placed on a tree limb that is attached to a woodsy base with dirt and leaves, or attached directly to a piece of driftwood that can be hung on the wall.

Most shoulder mounts will either be hung alone or attached to a panel. But a life-sized mount should be attached to a base with elements from its natural habitat. The options are endless, but the most common setting is probably a woodsy base with dirt, leaves, and ground clutter. A natural setting will add that last minor element of realism to your mount, so plan it carefully.

The authentic touches you add to a base can really make
a mount stand out.

Rock bases are also popular. You can make them by applying a
rock-base material to a skeletal structure of wood, or you can purchase them pre-made. Most rock bases designed and built by the
taxidermist can also be colored to enhance the qualities of the individual mount.

Think of the terrain or ground cover that was in the area where
the animal was taken. One good way to start is by making a dirt base
and then adding to it one element at a time—leaves, pine needles
or cones, small flowers, or ferns.

MAKING A NATURAL DIRT BASE

For our dirt base, we're going to work with a bobcat-sized animal in
a walking pose. Start with a piece of plywood. Thickness isn't as important as straightness; the materials you add will strengthen the

Trimming the plywood core for a dirt base.

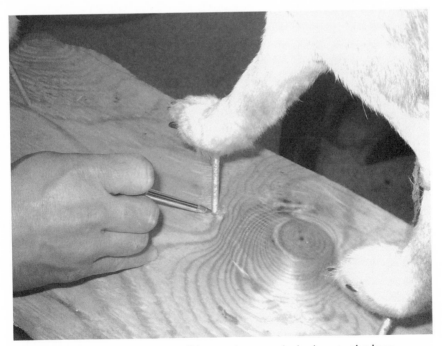

Mark points for the holes that will be used to attach the legs to the base.

Materials needed for base building include two-part foam, core material, and a preferred covering—dirt, rock, moss, etc.

plywood. Also, the plywood will be completely covered, so don't bother treating it with anything before you begin.

Cut the plywood in an oval shape that measures roughly 32 inches by 15 inches. This measurement is a basic guideline and can be adjusted slightly. Next, screw a 20-inch length of 1×6 to the center. This creates a core to which other materials can be attached. It's a good idea to place the holes for the leg rods or wires now to avoid damaging the foam you'll apply later on. Hold the mounted animal over the wood and mark each spot where a leg attachment makes contact. Drill the holes with a bit slightly larger than the rod or wire, then add base material.

The most popular base material is a two-part urethane foam. This is basically the same foam used in making manikins. When you purchase this foam for base building, however, it will be in liquid form. Mixing the two parts together creates a chemical reaction that causes the foam to expand and then harden. Directions come with each kit and these will include details on mixing and potential hazards.

Once the foam is mixed and begins to rise it will become very hot and sticky. Wear gloves and an apron when you apply the foam, as it can be very difficult to get off your hands. Also, be careful not to get any foam in areas where you don't want it.

It may take a few tries to get comfortable using the right amount of foam. To avoid waste, use the same size plywood each time and vary the formula slightly until you get just the right amount. Then keep a record of the type of animal being mounted, the size of the base, and the ingredients needed for each base. This will speed up any future base-building projects.

Lay the plywood core onto a shallow bed of peat moss. (Any type of dirt will work, but I like peat moss because of its price and availability.) The peat moss will prevent the foam from sticking to your workbench as it's applied.

The two foam components have complex names so they are simply dubbed "A" and "B." For proper expansion and hardening it is best to use a scale or other measuring unit to portion out each liquid. The foam is generally mixed 50/50. Use a cordless drill with a wire in the chuck that has been bent into the shape of a "P." With

Mixing foam with a cordless drill and a bent piece of wire.

If powdered tempera isn't available, a small amount of liquid paint will work nearly as well.

the drill spinning slowly, mix the liquids thoroughly until they begin to change colors and rise. You should learn to easily recognize the stage prior to expansion.

For smooth, even coverage it is sometimes best to apply the foam just seconds before expansion; experimentation will be the best teacher. Once it has hardened, if nothing else has been added, the foam will become a very light tan color, almost the color of a manikin.

Any particles that drift down from the mount will be easy to see against a light background like this, so it's usually a good idea to darken the foam. To add color to the foam prior to mixing the liquid components, pour in one or the other and add two teaspoons of powdered tempera paint to eight ounces of foam mixture. A variety of colors are available, but for dirt scenes a simple brown usually works best. Now mix the powdered tempera thoroughly into the chosen liquid. Once you achieve a uniform color, add the remaining component. Mix thoroughly until the foam begins to rise.

Pour the rising foam mixture onto the plywood core. It will be necessary to work quickly. Begin shifting the plywood side-to-side

Pour the foam mixture onto the plywood core.

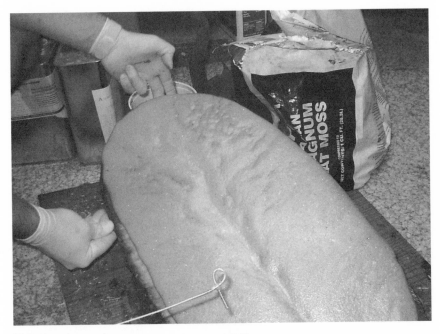

Shift the plywood to ensure proper coverage.

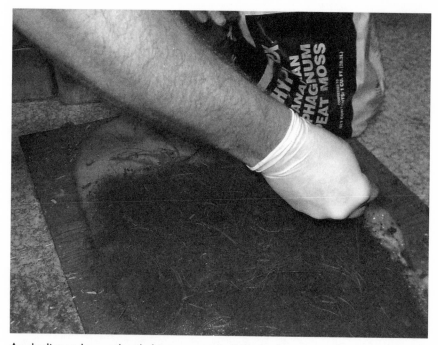

Apply dirt and any other habitat material while the foam is in the curing process, as this aids with adhesion.

and front-to-back; this will evenly distribute the foam and leave a smooth surface.

After the foam has been spread evenly, and before it dries, sprinkle dry peat moss onto the base. Adding pine needles will also enhance an otherwise plain dirt base. Be careful not to touch the foam surface while applying these materials. The surface will remain sticky for several minutes until the foam begins to harden. Once it does, the sprinkled-on dirt and most of the pine needles will be permanently attached.

Let the base sit undisturbed until hard to the touch. If the foam has been mixed properly, hardening should take place in less than twenty minutes.

Next, insert a short length of wire—one that matches the size of the leg wires—through each preexisting hole from the bottom. Push the wire straight through the foam, then gently wiggle to slightly widen the holes to accommodate the attachment rods or wires.

Remove the short length of wire and work each leg wire into the proper hole. It may take some maneuvering to find each hole, but be patient and the wire will soon slide through. When the wires are all started in the holes, push the feet flush with the base.

Bend each wire at a 90-degree angle against the bottom of the base, making sure that all four feet are snugly in place. Secure the mount to the base with 1½-inch screws (adjacent to the wire and through the same hole). This should firmly anchor the mount. Cut the excess wire and grind or sand off any sharp points. The screws should be flush with the bottom of the base, but if you would like to cover them, hot glue a small piece of felt over this area.

To further accentuate the base, attach any other vegetation or additives you think appropriate. Additions might include shed antlers, skulls, smaller animals, freeze-dried insects, arrows inserted into the foam as if they'd been shot, rocks, and so on. But try not to make the base too busy, as this may detract from the overall appearance of the mount.

If you would like to have a base with a finished hardwood frame you can build it yourself or purchase one from a panel or frame shop. These base frames are also available from most taxidermy suppliers.

We sized our base for a bobcat, but determining the appropriate base size for any animal is easy. Stand the mount on whatever base material you have chosen (again, plywood is probably the most common material). Make marks on the plywood approximately two to three inches wider than the animal's stance all the way around the base. Connect these and cut out your base.

This is just a good general guideline, however, as you may settle on a larger or smaller base for your individual mount. When I first started out I preferred larger bases, but as my experience grew I began to appreciate the ease, simplicity, and less distracting qualities of a smaller base.

MAKING A ROCK BASE

Rock bases are popular among taxidermists. For one thing, they are very easy to make and can also be purchased through most taxidermy catalogs. And, as most animals are medium to dark in color, the addition of a contrasting, light-colored base often enhances the mount.

Most commercial rock bases are re-created almost perfectly—great color and texture without the weight. Many are manufactured from a resin or fiberglass material, which makes them very durable.

The only drawback to commercially produced replica rock is their universal design. They will fit nearly all form positions closely but not perfectly. Some rocks are even designed for a particular type and position of manikin. However, for varied mount positions that aren't available with specific commercial bases, you must have the base custom-made or build it yourself. Don't worry, though, because building a nice-looking custom rock base isn't difficult.

First, you must decide whether to go with a wall mount or a floor mount.

Rocks for Floor Mounts

Cutting out a plywood core and then placing staples randomly across the plywood is the simplest way to make a rock base. The staples help secure the rock material to the plywood. Next, mix the rock material and spread it evenly across the base. If you are unable to find suitable rock material, a 50/50 mix of vermiculite and plaster will do the job. Spread this mix evenly and then use a sponge to texture the base. Finish by attaching the mount.

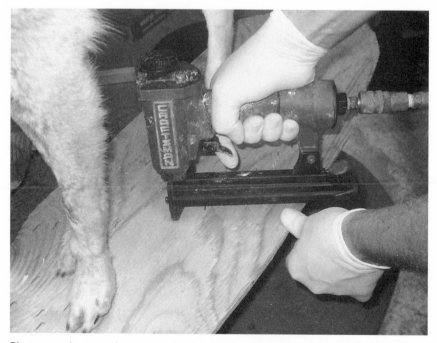

Placing staples into the plywood will help the rock mix adhere to the base.

Mix rock material thoroughly.

Spread rock mix onto the plywood core.

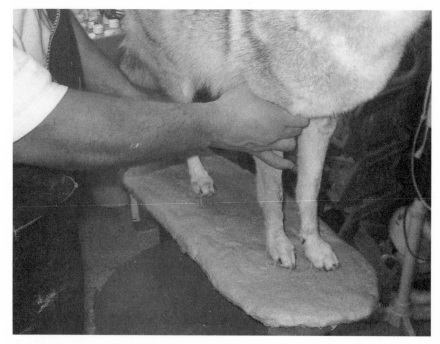

Attach the mount to the base.

For a nicer floor-mounted rock base, I most often use a rectangular shape rather than the oval shape I like to use with a dirt scene. Once again, this is purely personal preference, as rock bases can be built in any shape you desire. (I have yet to see a guideline for the shape of a rock.) If you want to include hardwood framing around your rock base it is usually best to make or buy the framework first then erect the skeletal structure to which the rock material will be attached.

Start by cutting a piece of plywood slightly larger than what I recommended for a general dirt base, maybe a couple of inches wider per side. Then begin attaching small, short pieces of wood (1×1s or 1×2s work great) to the areas where the feet will be attached. Screw in matching lengths of wood to either side of where the rod or wire holes will be; there should be two for each leg that will be connected to the base. The lengths of these pieces of wood will determine the size of the finished rock. The longer the pieces, the taller the rock will be upon completion.

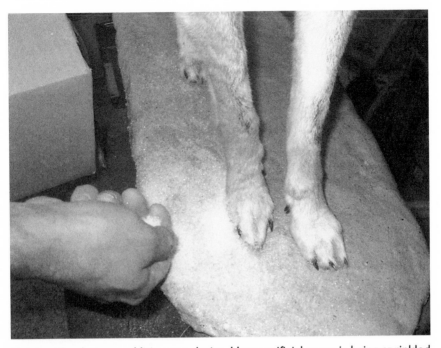

Finish with whatever additive you desire. Here artificial snow is being sprinkled on the base.

Next, attach a small piece of plywood that connects the two pieces securely at the top. Once each pair of wood strips has been attached to one another, drill a hole into the small piece of plywood similar in size to the rod or wire that will be used to attach the mount to the base. Adjust the length of the attachments until the mount stands in a balanced position. For example, if the mount were supposed to appear on flat ground it would look awkward if it appeared to be moving up or downhill.

The skeleton, or foundation, of the rock has no set pattern or definite rules of construction, other than that the attachment points should be strengthened to prevent a collapse. Start by cutting pieces of wood to various lengths. These pieces can be almost any size from ½×1 to 2×2. Thicker pieces of wood are unnecessary and will only add weight to the base. On the other hand, strips that are too thin may not be strong enough to properly support the mount or the overlying material. Attach these strips at various angles over the entire base.

Once the underlying support pieces have been attached, begin adding screen material over the entire base. This screen will be the preliminary surface, so now is the time to give your rock the shape you want. Attach the screen with a staple gun, stapling anywhere there is a wooden support. It is important to entirely cover the wooden structure, leaving no gaps. However, the predrilled holes should be left unobstructed so the legs of the mount can be attached without additional cutting or drilling once the base is complete.

Screen works well for creating the basic shape of the rock because it is flexible and porous, which helps it adhere to the actual rock material. Some taxidermists prefer to use chicken wire with an overlying burlap material that has been dipped in plaster. This method also works well, but it requires an extra step, and the plaster-laden burlap adds weight.

There are several quality brands of rock material available through taxidermy suppliers. As with many other aspects of taxidermy, you'll just have to work with a few until you find a favorite. Mix the material according to directions. Begin applying the material to the screen by hand, gently smoothing it out as you go. Thickness can vary and no set rules apply, but if you're concerned about weight keep the thickness near ¼ inch. This is usually thick enough to resist cracking.

When you've covered the entire base with rock material, start texturing the surface. Do this with a dampened sponge. Dab, rub, and rake the rock material until you achieve a natural appearance. Once the surface is completely textured, you have two options: wait until the rock material is completely dry to apply the desired coloring or continue the coloring process while the surface is wet. The rock material I use seems to absorb coloration better prior to drying, but experimentation will help you figure out your own preference.

If you study the colors of real rocks you will quickly see that they vary widely. But no rock will be only one color. Basic rock colors include various shades of brown, black, gray, and even green.

The easiest way to apply these colors is with a spray bottle filled with powdered tempera paint mixed with water. Spray coloring generously on one small area at a time until you get used to the procedure. After applying each color, lightly wipe the area with a sponge. This should imitate the varied colors found within natural rocks. An excellent way to produce natural colors is to apply different colors over the rock material one at a time.

When the base has dried completely, attach the mount. The attachment points should have remained open so begin by inserting the wires or rods into the preexisting holes. Then secure the mount by attaching and tightening the nuts onto the threaded rods exiting the legs, or by placing a ½-inch to 1-inch screw next to the attachment wire in each hole. One good way to gain access to these attachment points is to pre-cut small "doors" in the bottom of the base that will be hidden by the rock material above when the base is placed on the floor.

Rocks for Wall Mounts

A wall-hanging rock base is very similar to a floor base with one obvious exception: It will be attached to a wall. Instead of the underlying framework going upward from the base (as with a floor base) it must extend out from side and be strong enough to hold the mount for which it is being built.

Cut a piece of plywood to the size and shape of the intended base. Instead of using a square base, I prefer to cut slight angles into the backboard, as I have never seen a rock that was completely square or rectangular. The same shapes should be given to the rest of the base.

Once the general shape of the backboard is set, cut access holes through the back that will let you reach the attachment points. It is also best to attach hangers to the back at this time. Position at least one hanger on each side of the backboard so the base will balance easily. Also, place the hangers on the same level and record the distance between them. This will make it easier to place the screws in the wall on which the mount will hang.

Next, start attaching 1×2s perpendicular to the backboard. These will be used to attach the mount, so they should be long enough to position the mount away from the wall. Screw through the backboard and into the end of each 1×2; using two screws per piece will help anchor them securely. Brace each 1×2, as they'll need a lot of support.

Now attach the rest of the wood strips that will form the underlying structure of the rock. When these are secure, staple on the screen and rough out the shape; cover with rock material; and apply coloring just like you would for a floor base. Finally, reach through the back of the backboard and secure the mount through the attachment points.

The mount should sit perfectly in place, or close to it. If for some reason the mount sits slightly out of level or if a foot doesn't completely hide an existing hole, attach moss to the rock. Moss occurs naturally on many rocks, so adding it as cover can actually enhance the base. It's a great tool for covering imperfections or adding height to a low attachment spot. Attach it where it is needed with any all-purpose glue. Even if you don't need it to hide mistakes, moss or small brush that occurs naturally in and around rock crevices can greatly enhance a well-constructed but bland base.

Once it's leveled and attached to the wall, you should have a trophy that will provide a lifetime of fond memories.

CHAPTER

12

Mount Care

All too often I have customers come into my taxidermy shop to complain about the mounts their last taxidermist completed for them. The leading gripe seems to be that their deer or small game mounts only hold up for four or five years before beginning to deteriorate rapidly. As I'm always curious about the methods other taxidermists use, I usually begin asking for details. Often, I find that the mount in question had been placed near or over a heat source. This is a very poor location for any kind of mount. The only person at fault for the inevitable result is the owner who didn't take the time to learn the dos and don'ts of mount care.

By now all of your research, hard work, and investment in equipment should have paid off in some way. The fruit of your labor may only be a squirrel mount. Or you may have completed a variety of more complex small game mounts. Either way, you're going to want the artwork you create to be around for many years. Whether this happens or not, though, is entirely up to you. Proper care and cleaning are the keys.

The first rule for extending the life of a mount is to keep it away from a direct heat source. When a mount is subjected to extreme temperature changes it will quickly break down due to the expansion and shrinkage that takes place. And if the heat happens to be a dry heat, such as that from an electric heat source, the problems seem to compound quickly because any moisture that still exists in the mount will be pulled out. This moisture in a preserved skin is minute, but essential. If it is removed, the mount will become more like a potato chip than a well-preserved skin. This severe drying will eventually cause cracking and related damage.

By the same token, excessive moisture also creates a harmful environment for a mount. Many times, the hunter will return home

With all the hard work and expense that goes into harvesting and mounting a trophy, it would be a shame to not take care of it properly.

from the taxidermy shop with a beautiful mount only to be directed to a damp basement or garage. This direction usually comes from a non-hunting spouse who doesn't understand the hunter's desire to properly preserve, store, and display his or her trophy. Frankly, there isn't much you can do to combat this attitude, beyond trying to get your spouse involved in some of your outdoor adventures. If you introduce someone to the wonders of the outdoors they should soon learn to appreciate the beauty of most any wildlife art.

Not long ago I had a visit from a customer who had faced this exact predicament. He told me about an unbelievable elk hunt that he had been fortunate enough to take. After several days of trekking through rugged mountains he earned the opportunity to harvest a trophy bull. One well placed shot later and the photos showed the hunter smiling ear to ear. He was careful to follow good field-care guidelines and to prep the skin for the return home.

He visited a local taxidermist and arranged to have his trophy preserved and mounted. Months passed before he received the eagerly awaited phone call. He quickly made the trip to the taxidermist to pick up his trophy. The bull was a 6×6 that happened to score around 320, easily the trophy of a lifetime. But when he got home he was shocked to find that his wife adamantly refused to have such a beautiful creature grace any wall of their house.

In the interest of domestic tranquility the hunter placed his trophy in an outside utility building. But throughout the year the humidity and temperature within the brick building fluctuated like a yo-yo.

In three short years the tear ducts and nose pad had begun to crack. Needless to say, the mount was ruined. Had the hunter known that a stable environment was essential, he could at least have placed the mount at a friend's house until better arrangements could be made.

The ideal temperature and humidity range for a mount is similar to our own comfort range. Severe fluctuations in either should be strictly avoided.

Another major issue is the effect that the sun can have on a mount. Over time, direct sunlight is detrimental to almost everything, mounts

Display your mount in a controlled environment and away from direct sunlight.

included. The usual results are cracks due to regular heating and cooling. Another dead giveaway of sun damage is the severe fading that can, and will, eventually take place.

This can be easily avoided, of course, by simply taking a few precautions. If possible, situate the trophy away from any large south-facing windows. If this is impossible, at least try to restrict the sunlight with a blind or curtain. This will help tremendously.

Although controlling a mount's environment is ninety-nine percent of caring for it, you may eventually have to deal with a broken ear or body part. The mount may fall from a wall, or a child or pet may cause such damage while innocently roughhousing. Like most works of art a mount is fragile; so it's a good idea to locate it in a visible but out-of-the-way area. Still, mishaps are going to occur now and then.

Use wire, pins, and super glue to reattach the broken piece. Since areas such as the legs and tail have internal wiring that may still be attached, fixing a break may be as simple as repositioning the broken piece. Then you can further strengthen the affected area with glue and pins. If you proceed carefully and groom the damaged area you may be able to totally conceal the break.

Trophies also need to be dusted on a regular basis, and a vacuum can be used on most mammal mounts. Probably the most common method of dusting a mount is to simply wipe it with a damp cloth. How often your mount will need to be cleaned will depend heavily on its environment. Some homes seem to be dusty the day after a cleaning, while others don't show serious dust buildup for months at a time.

Be sure to clean the eyes well whenever you dust. The eyes play a vital role in the quality of a mount, and a dull, dusty eye can detract from an otherwise beautiful trophy. Wipe each eye thoroughly with a moistened cotton swab followed by a dry one.

Taxidermy suppliers also have a variety of products available that aid in shining and cleaning the hair or fur on a mount. Most produce a pleasant smell, something akin to leather. Avoid using a regular household cleaner.

With proper care and an ideal environment your hard-earned trophy will last longer than you do.

CHAPTER 13

Tips for Producing a Better Mount

Almost anyone who follows the directions provided in this book will be able to preserve and mount an animal. But if you want to achieve the most natural and lifelike works of art— as an occupation or just a hobby—you will have to study continuously and devote a great deal of time to your craft.

Throughout my years as a taxidermist I have learned many lessons the hard way. Some were obvious after the fact, others not so much. What follows are the best tips I can provide to help you avoid such pitfalls. Sure, you'll run into other obstacles if your stay in the world of taxidermy is a long one, but hopefully this advice will allow you to bypass many of the most common ones.

CHOOSE THE CORRECT MANIKIN

Choosing the correct manikin may seem like child's play. But many beginners—and even trained taxidermists—insist on using a form that is too large for the skin. The thought process seems to be that bigger is better. Most times, though, using a larger-than-necessary manikin only creates more problems.

Another problem that I ran into early on was choosing a pose with no regard to measurements. I had taken my first bobcat and wanted to mount it right away. Although I had spent considerable hours skinning, sewing, and helping with the mounting process, I had never been responsible for the entire operation from start to finish. So the first thing I did was pick up the taxidermy supply catalog and choose a pose. Size didn't matter—all bobcats are the same size, right? Wrong.

After several frustrating hours of stretching and pulling the skin and cutting and whittling the form, I decided it would be much easier to just order the correct manikin size. From then on I took accurate measurements for each animal to be mounted *before* ordering the manikin.

DEALING WITH DAMAGED AREAS

As I stated in the opening chapter, it is usually better to determine the pose you want before pulling the trigger. Sometimes, though, you have to no choice but to decide after the shot. If serious damage is done to an animal, the hunter may have to settle on a different pose that will effectively cover up the problem area. For example, if heavy damage is done to one side only, you may choose to mount the animal with the damaged side to the wall or cover it by placing the animal in a prone position.

If the animal received extensive body damage, a half mount or shoulder mount may be the only options. Maybe the raccoon you harvested has a damaged leg, in which case you may have to display the animal with its paw in a hollow log to simulate the animal's inquisitiveness, or search for food. Or maybe you can get away with just attaching grass or brush around the leg to hide the damage. The possibilities are endless; just use your imagination.

Keep in mind that nothing is really a lost cause if you're willing to consider all options. For instance, the hunter we discussed in the first chapter who shot his bobcat in the head didn't go home with a full-sized mount, but he did have the skin tanned. The spotted pelt still made a beautiful addition to his home.

Some problem areas may take care of themselves if the skin is cleaned and degreased properly. These elements can't be stressed enough. Proper cleaning eliminates hair that is dull or that clumps together. And once the taxidermist reaches the mounting stage, the skin and hair of his specimen should be clean to the touch without any blood or dirt residue.

Degreasing is just as important as proper cleaning, particularly if you choose dry preservative for your mount or decide to mount a greasy skin like a raccoon. It will help to shine the hair and will eliminate the possibility of any grease bleeding through to stain the hair later.

If your skin is in rough shape, a commercial tannery may be worth the investment, as they'll professionally clean and degrease it for you. You may even find that areas you thought were damaged just needed special care.

SEAMS

There's no way around it, taxidermy requires a lot of sewing. Poor, sloppy sewing can be the downfall of an otherwise great mount. To avoid this with your mounts, make sure that all seams are tight and well placed. The seam that is used most often in commercial taxidermy—which is any taxidermy not for competition—is a baseball stitch. To complete this stitch, tie one end of the thread off securely with a couple of overhand knots. Then insert the needle through the underside of the skin, bring it out the hair side, and cross over and repeat for the opposite side. In through the skin side, out from the hair side.

Keep the stitches as short and tight as possible and tie each end off securely and your seams should be fine. Once the seam is complete, tap it lightly with a small hammer to help flatten it. It also may help to brush the hair flat in its natural direction and then tack a small piece of cardboard over the seam. This will prevent the hair along the seam from standing on end as the skin dries.

BRING THE MOUNT TO LIFE WITH ACTION

After a lengthy study of reference materials, you will find that putting motion—no matter how small—into a mount can drastically improve its look. Most novice taxidermists are hesitant to put too much movement into their mounts. You often see this in the form of a straight, rigid tail.

But most animals are constantly portraying emotion through their tail positions. A dog's tail, for example, wags when he is happy and is tucked tightly under his body when he's scared. The same is true for most wild animals. Anyone who studies reference photos will pick up on this, yet a lot of new taxidermists are still afraid to move anything around. Sometimes you just have to go for it; you'll achieve the best results by trying different positions.

Once you learn to use facial expression and ear position to create an authentic mood you'll be able to choose from a wide range of poses.

The ears give you another opportunity to impart a lifelike appearance. I've seen many mounts with both ears in a forward, straight position. This is fine for statues, but most animals are constantly monitoring their surroundings. They swivel their ears, sometimes one at a time. Or they put both to the rear. Scared or aggressive animals pull their ears tight to their heads. A mount that portrays movement with the ears will be much more convincing.

Frankly, this goes for virtually every portion of the body. A mount I saw recently is a good example. It was a bobcat that was leaping for a bird. The mounting job itself wasn't extraordinary, but the tail appeared to be moving to one side and the ears were laid back in an aggressive posture. These small touches added realism to the mount, as if the cat were actually in motion.

As you learn more about taxidermy, you'll loosen up and gain confidence in your ability to re-create wildlife as naturally as possible.

Duplicating natural movement will really bring your mount to life.

Attach the Feet to the Base Before They Are Dry

As your taxidermy skills progress, you'll find yourself paying more attention to detail. One of these details, which I think many taxidermists overlook, is attaching feet to a base. Even after all the hard work that goes into a nice mounting job, a taxidermist will often attach the trophy to a flat board while it dries and then expect it to look as if it were walking along naturally when joined to the final base. But to achieve a natural stance, the feet need to conform to the surface on which they will be mounted. In a nutshell, the problem is that the taxidermist has allowed the animal to dry on one surface then attached it to another.

To avoid this with your mount, prepare the final base *prior* to mounting, and then attach the animal before it dries. Sometimes the taxidermist can get away with building the base to suit the critter, but for the best results you should conform the feet to the pre-made base. Little things like this can make or break an otherwise well-made mount.

Be Confident

In talking to other taxidermists, whether veterans or newcomers, it seems that their biggest disadvantage isn't lack of knowledge but the lack of confidence. Those without confidence are much more likely to let frustration and obstacles stop them from completing projects. Remember, though, that every taxidermist—no matter skilled—has had to fight through the same learning stages, the frustrations, the doubts. And I can assure you that the taxidermist who wins next year's world, national, or even state championship is struggling today to produce his best possible work. His first attempt won't be remotely similar to the one that clinches the prize.

When the going gets tough and you feel like taxidermy isn't for you, just quit—but not for good. Step away for a short breather to gather your thoughts, and then come back to the plate for another swing. Things will get easier and your work will improve. And when your project is finished you will have produced something beautiful with the added satisfaction that always comes from working hard to make something with your own two hands.

JOIN YOUR STATE TAXIDERMY ASSOCIATION

Taxidermy associations around the country hold annual seminars and competitions that are geared towards improving the techniques and craftsmanship of their members. Participating in these events and being able to ask other taxidermists in your area for advice can be invaluable.

In years past, taxidermy was basically a secret art. No books were written, no videos made, and you wouldn't have even thought of asking the taxidermist down the street for instruction. But times have changed. Joining a state taxidermy association can bring the wisdom of fellow taxidermists as close as a phone call away. Most are happy to provide how-to instruction to a fellow member. This is especially true if they know you are new to the art.

The competitions these organizations hold are also a tremendous learning tool. Some of the best taxidermists in the world will be there to critique your entry, and the advice they'll provide for improving your skills will be very helpful.

Check with one of the major taxidermy suppliers for information on contacting your own state association.

SUBSCRIBE TO TAXIDERMY MAGAZINES

Subscribing to a taxidermy magazine like *Breakthrough* or *Taxidermy Today* can be a tremendous asset. Although they are not geared solely toward small game taxidermy, much of their content is devoted to this subject. The articles written for these publications include the most advanced taxidermy procedures you'll find anywhere.

Call 1-800-783-7266 to contact *Breakthrough,* or 1-800-851-7955 to contact *Taxidermy Today.*

APPENDIX

Taxidermy Suppliers

Van Dyke's
P.O. Box 278
Woonsocket, SD 57385–0278
1-800-843-3320 or 605-796-4425
www.vandykestaxidermy.com

WASCO
1306 West Spring Street
P.O. Box 967
Monroe, GA 30655
1-800-334-8012 or 770-267-3625
www.taxidermy.com
wasco@taxidermy.net

Jim Allred Taxidermy Supply
216 Sugarloaf Road
Hendersonville, NC 28792
1-800-624-7507 or 704-692-5846
www.jimallred.com
allred@a-o.com

Research Mannikins
P.O. Box 315
Lebanon, OR 97355
1-800-826-0654 or 541-451-1538
www.rmi-online.com
rmi@rmi-online.com

McKenzie Taxidermy Supply
P.O. Box 480
Granite Quarry, NC 28072
1-800-279-7985; 1-888-279-7985
www.mckenziesp.com/
mcktaxid.asp
taxidermy@mckenziesp.com

Jonas Supply Company
21850 Dogwood Street
Louisville, CO 80027
1-800-525-6379 or 303-466-3377
www.jonastaxidermy.com
jonastaxidermy@worldnet.att.net

John Rinehart Taxidermy
   Supply Co.
A McKenzie Company
P.O. Box 480
Granite Quarry, NC 28072
1-800-279-7985; 1-888-279-7985
www.taxidermyonline.com
JRManikin@aol.com

Noonkester Taxidermy Supply
21452 Gravel Lake Road
Abingdon, VA 24211

1-800-888-3706 or 540-628-7182
www.noonkester.com
info@noonkester.com

Foster Taxidermy Supply
5124 Troy Highway
Montgomery, AL 36116
1-800-848-5602

Ben Mears Taxidermy & Supply
P.O. Box 131
223 Lake Road
Mantachie, MS 38855
1-800-257-2825 or 662-282-4594
www.mearstaxidermyandsupply.
  com
info@mearstaxidermyandsupply.
  com

Hide and Beak Supply Company
7887-B Highway 2
Saginaw, MN 55779
1-800-777-7916 or 218-729-8452
www.hidebeak.com
hidebeak@cpinternet.com

Authentic Taxidermy & Supply
3568 Lamar Avenue
Memphis, TN 38118
901-365-8101
www.AuthenticTaxidermy.com
info@authentictaxidermy.com

Matuska Taxidermy Supply
  Company
2678 Hwy 71
Spirit Lake, Iowa 51360
1-800-488-3256

www.matuskataxidermy.com/
  Pages/supply_company.htm
mattaxsupc@matuskataxi-
  dermy.com

Touchstone Taxidermy Supply
  Company, Inc.
5011 East Texas Street
Bossier City, LA 71111
1-800-256-4800 or 318-746-5792
members.aol.com/touchtxdmy
wtouchstn@aol.com

Rayline Mannikins, Inc.
A McKenzie Company
P.O. Box 480
Granite Quarry, NC 28072
1-800-279-7985; 1-888-279-7985
www.mckenziesp.com/
  mcktaxid.htm
taxidermy@mckenziesp.com

Joe Coombs Classics, Inc.
48555 Highway 445
Loranger, LA 70446
1-800-722-2327 or 985-542-2777
www.joecoombs.com
info@joecoombs.com

Dixieland Taxidermy Supply
9605 U.S. Highway 64
Somerville, TN 38068
1-800-465-4577 or 901-465-2345

Trufitt Life Form Mannikins, Inc.
1724 South Redwood
Salt Lake City, UT 84104
1-800-874-7660

INDEX